MANIFESTO FOR LIVING IN THE ANTHROPOCENE

MANIFESTO FOR LIVING IN THE ANTHROPOCENE

Katherine Gibson, Deborah Bird Rose, and
Ruth Fincher, editors

punctum books ∗ brooklyn, ny

First published in 2015 by
punctum books
Brooklyn, New York
http://punctumbooks.com

punctum books is an independent, open-access publisher dedicated to radically creative modes of intellectual inquiry and writing across a whimsical para-humanities assemblage. We solicit and pimp quixotic, sagely mad engagements with textual thought-bodies, and provide shelters for intellectual vagabonds.

ISBN-13: 978-0988234062
ISBN-10: 0988234068

Before you start to read this book, take this moment to think about making a donation to punctum books, an independent non-profit press,

@ http://punctumbooks.com/about/

If you're reading the e-book, you can click on the image below to go directly to our donations site. Any amount, no matter the size, is appreciated and will help us to keep our ship of fools afloat. Contributions from dedicated readers will also help us to keep our commons open and to cultivate new work that can't find a welcoming port elsewhere. Our ad/venture is not possible without your support. Vive la open-access.

Fig. I. Hieronymous Bosch, *Ship of Fools* (1490-1500)

ACKNOWLEDGMENTS

The editors would like to acknowledge with gratitude the financial assistance offered by the Academy of Social Sciences in Australia that allowed us to organize the workshop where many of the ideas contained in this book were aired and refined.

Freya Mathews's essay, "*Strategia*: Thinking with or Accommodationg the World," is extracted and adapted from her chapter "Why Has the West Failed to Embrace Panpsychism?" in *Mind That Abides: Panpsychism in the New Millennium*, ed. David Skrbina (Amsterdam and Philadelphia: John Benjamins, 2009), 341–260.

The projects on which Margaret Somerville's essay is based were funded by the Australian Research Council.

TABLE OF CONTENTS

Manifesto for Living in the Anthropocene

Preamble

Humanity's actions have become a new planetary force with accelerating effects on the biosphere. This new era, known as the Anthropocene, calls for new ways of thinking and knowing, and for innovative forms of action.

We are a group of concerned social scientists and creative scholars who are moved to address the unique qualities of our contemporary world. In the Anthropocene, we are summoned to expand our understandings of ways to conjoin nature and culture, economy and ecology, and natural and social sciences. Already, thinkers among us are exploring ways of dismantling traditional separations. We aim to further and expand this work, identifying multiple pathways toward alternative futures.

Research for the Anthropocene must and will harness the creativity of human potential to reduce harm and promote a flourishing biosphere.

Thinking

We want to engage in life and the living world in an unconstrained and expansive way. Our thinking needs to be in the service of life—and so does our language. This means giving up preconceptions, and instead listening to the world. This means giving up delusions of mastery and control, and instead seeing the world as uncertain and yet unfolding. So our thinking needs to be—

- Curious;
- Experimental;
- Open;
- Adaptive;
- Imaginative;
- Responsive; and
- Responsible.

We are committed to thinking with the community of life and contributing to healing.

STORIES

Stories are important for understanding and communicating the significance of our times. We aim to tell stories that—

- Enact connectivity, entangling us in the lives of others;
- Have the capacity to reach beyond abstractions and move us to concern and action;
- Are rich sources of reflection; and
- Enliven moral imagination, drawing us into deeper understandings of responsibilities, reparative possibilities, and alternative futures.

RESEARCHING

While we continue our traditions of critical analysis, we are forging new research practices to excavate, encounter and extend reparative possibilities for alternative futures. We look and listen for life-giving potentialities (past and present) by charting connections, re-mapping the familiar and opening ourselves to what can be learned from what already is happening in the world. As participants in a changing world, we advocate—

- Developing new languages for our changing world;
- Stepping into the unknown;
- Making risky attachments; and
- Joining and supporting concerned others.

COLLEAGUES, WHEREVER YOU MAY BE, PUT YOUR RESEARCH TO WORK AND TAKE A STAND FOR LIFE!

Scholars Concerned for Life in the Anthropocene, Georges River, 8 February, 2010: Kay Anderson, Jenny Cameron, Thom van Dooren, Kelly Dombroski, Ruth Fincher, Katherine Gibson, Julie Graham, Lesley Instone, Kurt Iveson, Kumi Kato, Freya Mathews, Jacqui Poltera, Kate Rigby, Gerda Roelvink, Deborah Bird Rose, Margaret Somerville, Simon Wearne, Jessica Weir, Anna Yeatman.

"Sydney apple," Georges River, 2010. Photograph by Katherine Gibson.

Preface

Katherine Gibson, Deborah Bird Rose, and Ruth Fincher

In the moist heat of a Sydney February a group of concerned scholars gathered on the banks of the Georges River close to the University of Western Sydney, Bankstown. Amongst us there were key thinkers from the fields of Anthropology, Education, Human Geography, Philosophy, Science and Technology Studies, Sociology, Political Theory, Communications and Film. We gathered to consider an ethics for living in this new era of human driven climate change called the "Anthropocene." We wrote the Manifesto above.

A butterfly dropped the germ of the idea for this gathering onto fertile ground as it flitted over the heads of two of us some time ago in another beautiful bushland setting. Then we were gathered to farewell and bury feminist, ecologist, philosopher, Val Plumwood, our friend and colleague. As Val's eco-coffin was carefully lowered into the soil on her beloved Plumwood Mountain a white butterfly joined us. It hovered hesitatingly here and there over the crowd and then off it went into the forest. It left something beautiful—an energy and a courage to go on. We resolved to strengthen the tentative connections between Ecological Humanities and Community Economies scholars. Inspired by Val's life and practice our February gathering was held in a setting that invited the bush, rocks, birds and river to be part of a creative conversation. It was generously supported by the Academy of Social Sciences in Australia.

As we sat and reflected, walked and talked, and subsequently wrote and read to prepare this book it was the challenge Val posed, soon before her death, that has been uppermost in our minds. Val wrote:

> If our species does not survive the ecological crisis, it will probably be due to our failure to imagine and work out new ways to live with the earth, to rework ourselves and our high energy, high consumption, and hyper-instrumental societies adaptively ... . We will go onwards in a different mode of humanity, or not at all. (Plumwood 2007, 1)

That we need to go on in a "different mode of humanity" is not, for the authors collected here, at question. As a group we accept the premise that we live in an era of unprecedented and rapid environmental and social change. The recent 10,000 year history of climatic stability on Earth that enabled the rise of agriculture and domestication, the growth of cities, numerous technological revolutions, and the emergence of modernity is now over. We accept that in the latest phase of this era, modernity is unmaking the stability that enabled its emergence. Over the 21st century, severe and numerous weather disasters, scarcity of key resources, major changes in environments, enormous rates of extinction, and other forces that threaten life are set to increase. But we are deeply worried that current responses to these challenges are focused on market-driven solutions and thus have the potential to further endanger our collective commons.

Today public debate is polarized. On one hand we are confronted with the immobilizing effects of knowing "the facts" about climate change. On the other we see a powerful will to ignorance and the effects of a pernicious collaboration between climate change skeptics and industry stakeholders. Neither position nourishes our desire to address Val's question. Clearly, to us, the current crisis calls for new ways of thinking and producing knowledge. Our collective inclination has been to go on in an experimental and exploratory mode, in which we refuse to foreclose on options or jump too quickly to "solutions."

In this spirit we feel the need to acknowledge the tragedy of anthropogenic climate change. It is important to tap into the emotional richness of grief about extinction and loss without getting stuck on the "blame game." Our research must allow for the expression of grief and mourning for what has been and is daily being lost. But it is important to adopt a reparative rather than a purely critical stance toward knowing.

Might it be possible to welcome the pain of "knowing" if it led to different ways of working with non-human others, recognizing a confluence of desire across the human/non-human divide and the vital rhythms that animate the world? Our discussions have focused on new types of ecological economic thinking and ethical practices of living. We are interested in:

- Resituating humans within ecological systems;
- Resituating non-humans in ethical terms;
- Systems of survival that are resilient in the face of change;
- Diversity and dynamism in ecologies and economies;
- Ethical responsibility across space and time, between places and in the future; and,
- Creating new ecological economic narratives.

Starting from the recognition that there is no "one size fits all" response to climate change, we are concerned to develop an ethics of place that appreciates the specificity and richness of loss and potentiality. While connection to earth others might be an overarching goal, it will be to certain ecologies, species, atmospheres and materialities that we actually connect. We could see ourselves as part of country, accepting the responsibility not forgotten by Indigenous people all over the world, of "singing" country into health. This might mean cultivating the capacity for deep listening to each other, to the land, to other species and thereby learning to be affected and transformed by the body-world we are part of; seeing the body as a center of animation but not the ground of a separate self; renouncing the narcissistic defense of omnipotence and an equally narcissistic descent into despair.

We think that we can work against singular and global representations of "the problem" in the face of which any small, multiple, place-based action is rendered hopeless. We can choose to read for difference rather than dominance; think connectivity rather than hyper-separation; look for multiplicity—multiple climate changes, multiple ways of living with earth others. We can find ways forward in what is already being done in the here and now; attend to the performative effects of any analysis; tell stories in a hopeful and open way—allowing for the possibility that life is dormant rather than dead. We can use our critical capacities to recover our rich traditions of counter-culture and theorize them outside the mainstream/alternative binary. All these ways of thinking and researching give rise to new strategies for going forward.

Think of the chapters of this book as tentative hoverings, as the fluttering of butterfly wings, scattering germs of ideas that can take root and grow.

THINKING WITH OTHERS

1: THE ECOLOGICAL HUMANITIES

The ecological humanities is a new interdiscipline that has emerged specifically to address the fact that current ecological problems, including extinctions, climate change, toxic death zones, water degradation, and many others, are anthropogenic events. Acknowledging the reality of human agency, we are no longer in the position of being able to sustain the idea that humans are separate from nature. In Dipesh Chakrabarty's (2009) memorable words, in the wake of our awareness of anthropogenic climate change, the Western division between human history and natural history has now been breached.

In spite of this knowledge, actual practices that breach boundaries struggle for recognition. Within our universities, for example, the division between arts and sciences is reinforced as often as it is breached. At the same time, the need for dialogue with knowledge systems that never promoted a break between natural and human histories is radically enhanced. We are thus called to build dialogical bridges between knowledge systems: between ecological sciences and the humanities, between Western and other knowledge systems. The key point, expressed vividly by the philosopher Val Plumwood, is the need for new ways of imagining, being and becoming human:

> We struggle to adjust because we're still largely trapped inside the enlightenment tale of progress as human control over a passive and "dead" nature that justifies both colonial conquests and commodity economies. The real threat is not so much global warming itself, which there might still be a chance to head off, as our own inability to see past the post-enlightenment energy, control and consumption extravaganza we so naively identify with the good, civilized life to a sustainable form of human culture. The time of *Homo reflectus*, the self-critical and self-revising one, has surely come. *Homo faber*, the thoughtless tinkerer, is clearly not going to make it. We will go onwards in a different mode of humanity, or not at all. (Plumwood 2007, 1)

Plumwood's eloquent words are a recent contribution to what has been a continued call for cultural change throughout the second half of the twentieth century. Aldo Leopold, for example, in his famous 1949 article on the land ethic, wrote of the need for a new concept of community, one that would include the whole of the biotic community (including humans) within a domain of ethics. The great ecologist Paul Shepard wrote in 1973 that, "It seems that in staring at the environmental crisis we have missed the central spark of ecology itself, its unexpected connections to the whole of life." He speaks briefly about the Western thinking that separates humanity out from the rest of the living world, backgrounded as "nature," and he concludes: "In the end what we are asked to do is reshape our image of man" (Shepard [1973] 1998, xxvi). Gregory Bateson was not so diplomatic. Working with the axiom that the unit of survival is organism and environment, he wrote:

> If you put God outside and set him vis-a-vis his creation and if you have the idea that you are created in his image, you will logically and naturally see yourself as outside and against the things around you. And as

you arrogate all mind to yourself, you will see the world around you as mindless and therefore not entitled to moral or ethical consideration. The environment will seem to be yours to exploit . . . If this is your estimate of your relation to nature *and you have an advanced technology*, your likelihood of survival will be that of a snowball in hell. (Bateson [1972] 1973, 436–437, italics in original)

The ecological humanities aims to work across the great divides in knowledge that have enabled us to sustain a faulty image of humanity, an image that holds humans apart, and in control.[1] We are not aiming to homogenize everything, or to suggest that everyone has to do or think everything. Quite the opposite, we acknowledge that there are many abrasive edges between knowledge systems. We believe that rubbing those abrasive edges together enables something new to happen. Paul Shepard wrote of the central spark of ecology; we are working toward sparks of knowledge. We are dedicated to ethical and critical analysis and encounter.

These are big issues, and there is always the danger of running off in all directions at once. Plumwood outlined two major tasks before us at this time: the first is to resituate the human in ecological terms, and the second is to resituate the non-human in ethical terms. To resituate the human in ecological terms is to overcome the idea that humans are outside of nature, and thus is the first step toward overcoming a humanities worldview that defines the human without reference to the living world. Along with the wider and more abstract issues, we are working to undermine the boundaries that have been deployed to hold humans separate from other animals. The second task—to resituate the non-human in ethi-

---

[1] See the Ecological Humanities website here: http://www.ecological humanities.org.

cal terms—overcomes the idea that the non-human world is devoid of meaning, values, and ethics. It is a first step towards overcoming a Western science worldview that defines the natural world as morally inert. In this endeavour, a major focus is on the widespread existence of sentience and agency amongst living beings, expressed vividly in the ethological work of Marc Bekoff in books such as *Minding Animals* (2002), and *Wild Justice* (Bekoff and Pierce 2009).

Each of the two tasks Plumwood identified works toward connectivity, and connectivity calls for its own non-linear recursive logic. It may be that stories are the most effective forms of communicating such densely complex logic. Steven Muecke (1997, 184–185) offers us the view that connection is a way of reasoning that leads us to commitment. He provokes us to decenter (not abandon) Cartesian rationality in favor of a more inclusive set of logics.

The logic of commitment in the context of Earth life is expressed with great integrity and beauty in many Indigenous knowledge systems. The Australian Aboriginal philosopher Mary Graham (2008) writes that indigenous cultures of land and place are based on two axioms: the land is the law; and you are not alone in the world. These two axioms can be heard as an indigenous ethic and practice of connectivity. The second axiom—you are not alone—situates humanity as a participant in a larger living system. The first—land is law—requires all living things to recognize and submit to the law of the living world.

Graham's enunciation of key axioms is extremely challenging. Knowledge developed from the axiom that the land is the law fundamentally reverses the idea that humans are in control. Similarly, knowledge developed from the axiom that you (we) are not alone brings us, as humans and as individuals, into face-to-face encounter with people, non-humans, places, ecosystems, and other biosocial communities where our presence has brought harm. Both axioms, therefore, bring us into serious discomfort and raise questions about the quality of dialogue that may be open to us.

The discomfort we feel as humans is dwarfed by the pain

that is being experienced across ecological systems. For Indigenous people whose lives and well-being are embedded within country, both as a matter of philosophy and as a matter of lived experience, the on-going devastation is violent. Phil Sullivan, a traditional owner of country along the Darling River in Bourke, speaks of the last line of defense. His thinking comes out of the disastrous colonization that did its best to ruin his people and his culture, and has done a great deal to wreck his country. He lives within the heart of the Western catastrophic push toward destruction. He has been there, his country is there, and he has had to work out what you hold on to when everything is collapsing. Respect, he says, is the last line of defense.

Respect is a matter of knowledge—of knowing the connections so that one knows the many contexts in which respect is due, and knowing how to look after things so that one can fulfill one's role in life. "The outward things may pass," Phil said, "but the respect, the thing inside, will last. We respect our animals and our land. That's what I call our last line of defense. The last line of defense is respect" (quoted in Rose, James, and Watson 2003, 67).

The logic of connection holds that the web of life is a web of mutual inter-dependencies. Human beings are enmeshed in webs of life as much as are koalas, eucalypts, flying foxes, coral, vultures and bacteria. The web of life really is Earth, because this is what Earth is—a place where life came into being and continues to come into being. Respect is an ethics of engagement with this place, our home; it is an ethics that brings gratitude for the gifts of life into dialogue with our responsibilities within the wider webs of life.

2: Economy as Ecological Livelihood

J.K. Gibson-Graham and Ethan Miller

Can we overcome our hyper-separation from the more-than-human world and take up membership in a thoroughly ecological community of life? While the demands of "the economy" are set in opposition to the needs of "the environment"; while the economy is seen as a vulnerable system that cannot accommodate allocations of social wealth to earth-repair and species protection without risking collapse; while the economic "we" continues to squander and ignore the gifts of the more-than-human world that gives us life, the answer seems to be a depressing "No." To answer "Yes" we must begin to rethink and re-enact the relationship between economy and ecology.

We have inherited a vision of "the economy" as a distinct sphere of human activity, marked off from the social, the political, and the ecological as a domain of individualized, monetized, rational-maximizing calculation. This economic sphere rests upon and utilizes an earthly base of (often invisible) ecologies that are swept up into its domain to become "resources," passive inputs for production and consumption measured primarily by their market value. Economy is "naturalized" in the sense that it is presented as a realm of objective, law-like processes and demands; yet this naturalization is at the same time a process by which the more-than-human world is affirmed as *external* to our economic lives, and the complexities of our interdependencies are rendered invisible and unaccountable. The economy thus assumes a presence and dynamism—manifest, for example, in the demand for endless growth—that appears to be independent from the living world upon which it depends.

This powerful and abstracted construction of the economy emerged from and enabled agricultural and industrial revolutions that gave rise to urbanization, increased standards of living for many, and vast and unprecedented mobilizations and transformations of energy and matter on the part of certain humans. But it also produced and legitimated tremendous violence and inequity, and has generated unforeseen impacts that are undermining the long-term viability of earthly survival not just for humans, but for myriad other species and more-than-human communities. Enabling as it has been for some, this view of economy-ecology relations now stands squarely in the way of imagining and enacting an ethics for living in the Anthropocene.

Recognizing "the economy" as a historical, discursive production rather than an objective ontological category (Mitchell 1998, 2008; Callon 2007) can enable us to begin exploring different ways of thinking and experiencing our processes of livelihood-making. What if we were to see economic activities not in terms of a separate sphere of human activity, but instead as thoroughly social and ecological? What if we were to see economic sociality as a necessary condition of life itself? What if we were to see the economy *as* ecology—as a web of human ecological behaviors no longer bounded but fully integrated into a complex flow of ethical and energetic interdependencies: births, contaminations, self-organizings, mergings, extinctions, and patterns of habitat maintenance and destruction?

Starting from this premise, we might begin to see the history of economic thought as a discursive enclosure of ecological space analogous to—and, in fact, historically parallel to—the material and legal enclosure of commons from the 16th century to the present (Perelman 2000). Just as the discourse of individual private property emerged with its legal rules of ownership, use and transfer, divorcing property (as a thing) from social relations, so the discourse of a separate economy evolved with and through terms, techniques and disciplinary practices that increasingly differentiated and distanced it from other spheres of human and non-human behavior and interaction. Economy, then, was produced when discursive boundaries, at once symbolic and material, were drawn around a particular configuration of ecological relationships—specifically those between certain humans and a world made into resources for their instrumental use. Diverse processes of human livelihood were reduced to narrow logics. Sociality was reserved only for those who count as "human." And all more-than-human life was relegated to the domain of passive objects.

By making a certain kind of sense of the world, this discourse of "the economy" literally *made sense*—transforming our sensual perceptions and experiences, altering the material and conceptual conditions of possibility for our identifications with others, and changing our abilities to see, think and feel certain inter-relationships and the responsibilities that come with such experiences.

Our challenge is to engage in forms of thought and practice that undermine the conditions of possibility for thinking "the economy" as a hyper-separated domain beyond the reach of politics, ethics and the dynamics of social and ecological interdependence. How might we cultivate genuinely ethical ecological-economic sensibilities? How might we reconfigure our notions of economy and ecology in ways that help us take responsibility for being alive together *as* life? We suggest three strategies that might bear some ethical fruit.

STRATEGY 1: RETHINKING BEING

For political theorist Jean Luc Nancy, the individual emerges from an essential sociality, rather than the other way around as is often conceived (2000, 44). He suggests that we replace the singular philosophical conception of "Being" with a "being-in-common" that does not reduce us to a unity or shared essence. For theorist of evolutionary biology Lynn Margulis, the process of symbiogenesis suggests that "individuals are all diversities of co-evolving associates" (quoted in Hird 2009, 65). Life does not exist without community as a process of connection-amidst-difference, without being-in-common. "Life," write Margulis and Sagan, "is an orgy of attractions" (Margulis and Sagan 1995, 157).

If we cease to think of ourselves as singular, self-contained beings and begin to think alongside, for example, the multiple communities of bacteria and bacterial symbionts from which we continually take shape and of which we are but fleeting, temporary manifestations (Hird 2009; Hird 2010); or if we place our activities in the context of the billions-of-years-old, emergent, planetary-scale process of biological self-construction known as "Gaia" (Lovelock 2000; Harding 2006; Volk 2003), it is no longer possible to identify a singular "humanity" as a distinctive ontological category set apart from all else.

What difference might it make if we accept that from the scale of Gaia, to the scale of the microscopic bacteria that form the laboring basis for nearly all biological energy production and transformation, there is a "we" bound together in myriad interrelationships that are themselves the very conditions of existence for our sense of a human "we"? Being-in-common—that is, *community*—can no longer be thought of or felt as a community of humans alone; it must become *multi-species community* that includes all of those with whom our livelihoods are interdependent and interrelated.

From this standpoint, there is no more ground for the construction of a human "economy" separate from its ecological context than there would be for ecologists to consider the provisioning practices of bees (see *fig. 1*) as an independent "system"—with its own internal laws and imperatives—wholly separate from their constitutive interrelationships with flowering plants, other pollinators, soil mycorrhizae, nitrogen fixing bacteria, seed dispersing birds and mammals. Human sociality is simply a particular manifestation of the mutual interrelationships between and among species and between and among communities of living beings that implicate lives ranging from the mitochondria in our cells to pollinators that make agriculture possible. If, to paraphrase Foucault, there is no "outside" to ecology (1980, 141), the big difference between those who *have* economy and those who *don't* is our symbolic capacity to *represent* ourselves as constituting a distinct sphere of existence in which sociality is reduced to individual desire. In other words, we are separate only by virtue of our ability to conceive of these separations.

Figure 1. Bee swarm. Photograph by Kate Boverman.

We might say, from a Gaian perspective, that we humans are a manifestation of the self-organizing processes of planetary life experimenting with particular forms of self-consciousness. Certainly this makes members of our species distinctive and allows us to generate previously impossible ecologies. But by thinking and building ourselves into self-conscious separation from ecological interrelationships and the sociality of life, we have made many of our livelihood processes into enemies of ecological resilience. Our acknowledgement of this history, and our commitment to rejoining a community of life through both our concepts and our actions is a crucial step toward a more robust ethical engagement with the world.

STRATEGY 2: REDEFINING ECONOMY

Let us try to think "economy" not as a unified system or a domain of being but as diverse processes and interrelations through which we (human and more-than-human) constitute *livelihoods.* "Economy" (*oikos*-habitat; *nomos*-negotiation of order) might then become a conceptual frame or theoretical entry point through which to explore the diverse specificities of livelihood creation by a population (members of the same species) or a community (multi-species assemblage). Economic analysis might then trace and track practices of community survival/management, including processes of co-existence and interdependence with all other populations or communities. Now, if we imagine the co-existence of diverse human economies, diverse salmon economies, diverse bee economies, diverse bacterial economies, and so on, along with the spatio-temporal community economies that they create together, "ecology" (*oikos*-habitat, *logos*-account of) becomes a conceptual frame from which to view the articulated whole of interacting diverse economies. The ecological entry point forces us to step back from the temporary centering operations of economics and ask how relations of livelihood creation and collective provisioning interact, conflict, co-constitute each other, and generate emergent properties.

Clearly such an approach would challenge us to rethink our places in the world, and to re-imagine the identities and social categories through which we've grown accustomed to view our interrelationships. What other differences can this redefinition make? For one, it might enable us to develop stronger conceptualizations of livelihood processes that are shared across species and from which we might have a great deal to learn. Jacobs' (2000) application of ecological concepts to regional economies, experimental practices of biomimicry (Benyus 2002), and the application of ecological wisdom through permaculture design (Mollison 1990; Holmgren 2002) are all examples of sites where the livelihood work of bees, grasses and bacteria become spaces of inter-species learning (see *fig. 2*).

Figure 2. Feeding time. Photograph by Kate Boverman

This redefinition might also offer pathways for developing more robust understandings of the complex interconnections between specific human livelihood practices and the more-than-human world from which they emerge (and which they transform). It might lead, for example, to a different analysis of the ethical and material implications of interdependence between diverse bee economies and diverse human agricultural economies—from the vast agri-business economy that promotes monoculture and dependence on the industrial reproduction of non-native pollinators (Mathews 2011a) to the integrated community farm that cultivates resilient polycultures of human, plant and bee life. When we begin to recognize that we are not alone in our livelihoods and that our human economies are inextricably linked with the economies of more-than-human others, might our ways of understanding and experiencing economic crisis, development and well-being begin to fundamentally shift?

STRATEGY 3: ETHICAL COORDINATES FOR MORE-THAN-HUMAN COMMUNITY ECONOMIES

We have redefined economy as ecology from the standpoint of actors constituting a community and producing livelihoods together, and ecology as the interactions of different diverse community economies. We arrive, then, at the ethical questions that lie at the heart of our economic and ecological relations: "How do we live together with human and non-human others?" Here we might turn to the work of identifying key sites of ethical negotiation—what we have elsewhere called the ethical coordinates of community economies (Gibson-Graham 2006, Ch. 4; Gibson-Graham and Roelvink 2010). Building on and adding to these, we suggest that an economic ethics for the Anthropocene calls us to become practiced in negotiating:

> PARTICIPATION: Who is the "we" that participates in the constitution of livelihoods and community economies? This involves cultivating forms of knowing and becoming that open us to the complexities of our interdependencies, to their animate interactions with us, and to the forms of responsibility this calls forth.

NECESSITY OR SUFFICIENCY: What do "we" need for survival? What constitutes "enough"? This includes asking about what is necessary for the dignified survival of all living beings and communities with whom we are interdependent, and about how we might *consume* in ways such that one species' or community's consumption does not compromise the survival chances of others.

SURPLUS: How do "we" produce, appropriate, distribute and mobilize surplus? Our new accounting must include surplus that is generated not just by human labor, but by the work of plants, animals, bacteria, fungi and dynamic energetic systems.

COMMONS: How do "we" make and share a *commons*, the material commonwealth of our community economies, with this new, more-than-human "we" in mind? Can we, for example, begin to see the chickens, bees and fruit trees of a cooperative farm not as part of that farm's commons (as shared resources), but rather as living beings participating in the co-constitution of the *community* that, together, *makes and shares the farm*?

Imagine an economics in which these kinds of questions were placed at the forefront of theory, public debate, and practical action—an economics in which the dynamics of livelihood were understood not in terms of a narrow range of monetized maximizing (human) activity unfolding according to the dictates of market forces, but as dynamics of appreciative inquiry into diverse forms of interdependence, complex relations of community-making, and ethical negotiations of multiple rationalities and ways-of-living. If community is what emerges as living beings make and share worlds together, then community economies are the sites where we imagine and struggle—as increasingly-attentive members of a community of life—to balance our needs with the needs of others, to account for and to offer recompense for the gifts of surplus we receive from the earth and earth others, and to begin to build together an ethical practice of economy for living in—and beyond—the Anthropocene.

3: LIVES IN CONNECTION

JESSICA K. WEIR

Climate change, spectacular in its scale and force, is the cumulative result of intertwined human and non-human agencies. It is perhaps the most profound expression of the earth's agency—the capacity of this world to act, to show its power in all our lives. The Anthropocene throws us a particular challenge to acknowledge those ecological connections that sustain our existence. We live within networks, webs, and relationships with non-human (or more-than-human) others, including plants, animals, rivers and soils. We rely on each other for food and fresh water. We are co-participants in what is happening and what will happen next. In southeast Australia where I live, we are told to expect hotter temperatures of longer duration, and more dramatic rain events—a combination that further extends the variability of our flood and drought cycles. In this already hot and arid country, where fresh water so clearly gives life, such changes will touch all.

Acknowledging our shared past, present and future with the many species and environments where we live is an intellectual counter to "separation thinking." Separation (or binary) thinking denies our co-produced realities, our life sustaining connections with sentient others, and leaves no grounds for us to engage with ecological life in ethical terms (Rose 1999). This is being addressed by an intellectual rethink underway in western knowledge systems, whereby humanity is being repositioned *within* nature (Ingold 2000, 42). In Australia, this intellectual rethink is also an intercultural conversation being had between Indigenous and non-Indigenous people. Indigenous people have inherited knowledge traditions from their ancestors and ancestral creators about how to live in Australia. Of great significance is the importance of place, or "country" as Indigenous people call their traditional lands (Kinnane 2002, 25). In its most expansive sense, country is much more than just territory, it is where knowledge comes from. Country is where the rules for existence and many of the relationships between species and humans were established by ancestral creative beings (Rose 2000 [1992], 43–44). This is a holistic knowledge tradition which emphasizes connections, respect and mutuality. Rather than mindless matter, the plants, animals and places have agency, law and language.

The interplay of separation thinking and connectivity thinking is evident in the intercultural discussions about water management in the Murray-Darling Basin in southeast Australia. The Murray and Darling Rivers extend west into the semi-arid and arid country, with extremely variable flows of water. Plants and animals have co-evolved with this variability, by breeding and taking advantage of food in the flood, and conserving water or living elsewhere to survive drought. In the nineteenth century, the colonial authorities and water entrepreneurs began planning to regulate this variable flow, to provide a more predictable and reliable water source. The fertile Murray River and its tributaries became the focus of inland settlement based on the diversion, storage, and allocation of river water for irrigated agriculture.

Alongside this agriculture and settlement, diverse Aboriginal peoples have survived the violence and opportunities of colonization to enjoy, maintain, transmit and revive their cultural inheritance, including their knowledge traditions. This is evident in the way Yorta Yorta people speak about their country, which has at its heart the Barmah-Millewa wetland. The Barmah-Millewa wetland is located amongst the slow, twisting folds of the Murray River, and supports Australia's largest river red gum forest (see *fig.* 1). Yorta Yorta Elder Henry Atkinson told me how, in the 1930s, his father and mother's father left the mission and lived in the forest by fishing for native fish, mussels, Murray crayfish and turtles (quoted in Weir 2009, 51). Henry expressed this as a relationship of the river caring for his people. Yorta Yorta man Lee Joachim describes the regenerative power of the Barmah-Millewa wetland as that of a kidney. The fresh river water flushes this kidney to regenerate country and people (quoted in Weir 2009, 13). Lee mixes kidneys and wetlands together in the intimacy of life.

Figure 1. Lee Joachim's children—Noah, McKenzie and Bonnie— standing under a river red gum in the Barmah Forest, Yorta Yorta country. Photograph by Jessica Weir. Reproduced with permission.

Yorta Yorta Elders have seen the regenerative capacity of the Barmah-Millewa wetland vastly diminish within their lifetimes. River regulation to reduce variable flows has reduced the ability of plants and animals to survive and thrive. Combined with the clearance of native vegetation, the introduction of weeds and pests, and other land use changes, the rivers are now in very poor health. Henry Atkinson used to drink from the fresh river water, now he would not even risk swimming in the Murray's muddy polluted flow (quoted in Weir 2009, 60). Cultural practices such as hunting, gathering and fishing have suffered. Because of the ties that bind people and country, Lee Joachim expresses the diminishment of the river as a threat to Yorta Yorta existence as a people.

Declining river health, and its effect on agricultural production, has challenged Australia's policy makers to acknowledge the damage of past water management and innovate ways to address river health (Murray-Darling Basin Authority 2010). Water policy is moving towards acknowledging the central importance of the rivers by introducing environmental water flows for river health. At the same time, Aboriginal people are developing their own water policies, which emphasize the rivers as the source of all life. "Cultural flows" is one of these policies. Cultural flows are an expression of how Aboriginal people would like to see water returned to the river country, and include ecology, history, culture, society, economy and more. There is currently a very interesting dialogue taking place between Aboriginal people and policy makers about cultural flows and environmental flows—what these flows mean, where they complement each other, and where they do not.

The realization of both environmental flows and cultural flows rests partly with whether we can reduce the powerful influence of separation thinking, and this is also what thwarts our ethics for living lives in connection. Cultural flows are quickly trapped in the contradictory constraints of separation thinking, and are more easily communicated as a narrowly defined water allocation (Weir 2009, 119–129). Environmental flows are cast by detractors as being at the expense of water for irrigation, playing into the binary which separates ecology and economy as oppositional goals. Surely the near death of the river country reveals that the future of our irrigation economics is entangled with river health. It is to our profound detriment, and to all the lives that we are entangled with, that we pretend we are managing and allocating a discrete resource, instead of admitting that we have been messing with a life source, within which our own lives are held. We need to move from thinking of our rivers and wetlands as resources for consumption, to thinking of them as being vital organs for our very existence.

Lee Joachim has described the Murray River as a living being which sustains itself and the lives of others (quoted in Weir 2009, 53–54). Lee encourages us to begin our ethics of connection by listening to country. Through listening, we become drawn into a communicative relationship with the river. Through communication we acknowledge the sentience and agency of ecology life. We extend subjectivity to place, plants, animals and rivers, and we lay the basis for love, care and ethics with non-human others (Ingold 2000, 69, 76; Rose 2004, 13). We find both the intellectual framework and the passion for restoring our relationships with fresh water, and we strengthen the life-giving connections we need for what lies ahead.

4: CONVIVIALITY AS AN ETHIC OF CARE IN THE CITY

RUTH FINCHER AND KURT IVESON

For some, the environmental pressures that have given birth to the Anthropocene are inextricably linked with two centuries of explosive urbanization. The voracious appetite of modernity is nowhere better illustrated than in our "vortex cities" (McManus 2005), which suck in food, water, and energy from elsewhere in ways which tend to mystify the connections between urbanized consumption of resources and the environments which support them. Likewise, the hubris of modernity is also always apparent in cities, with their infrastructures designed to dominate rather than respond and adapt to the environment—from the freeways slicing through neighborhoods and countryside to the re-engineering of rivers and harbors.

And yet, such accounts of cities are only partial. Even as they are characterized by all sorts of environmental and social problems, cities have also been fertile ground for collective experiments in generating new ethical practices of relating to one another and our environment. Such practices are worth reflecting upon, as they constitute a vital resource for efforts to construct better futures.

Precisely because cities are places of large population numbers and often high population density, it is almost impossible in a city to avoid some contact with other people, however inconsequential. This contact can be experienced in all manner of ways. In some places within urban environments, we see the potential for these encounters to be experienced as a kind of *conviviality* with strange others, viewing conviviality as the purposeful sharing of activities by individuals who may not necessarily be known to each other; interactions which are usually fleeting rather than sustained, and which are conceptually at some distance from sharing identities (Fincher and Iveson 2008). Consider the following everyday activities which are convivial and rely on the availability and nature of certain (primarily urban) physical settings in order to occur.

Our first example is the act of going to the library. Going to the public library is an activity of many urban inhabitants and visitors to cities. Libraries aren't just sites for borrowing books and DVDs, and then departing. Rather, in libraries we find people browsing through newspapers and magazines, studying, keeping warm or cool, checking and sending emails, reading to their small children, participating in book clubs and genealogical discussions. People pursue their interests in solitude or in groups with others, talk casually to librarians and other library users, and share a space with strangers. Public libraries have no entrance fee and few charges for their services. There is an air about them—they are places in which respect for others will occur, even without notices saying so and vigilant enforcement of this expectation. (Although this is sometimes sorely tested by mobile phone users!) Libraries are places, most often in cities, in which convivial, often fleeting, encounter across difference is the norm. Library users understand this and demonstrate their care by practicing conviviality in this space.

Playing in a temporary space on a city street is a second example. A growing band of writers is considering the ways that the spaces of cities accommodate the needs of children for convivial encounter. Some like Moss and Petrie (2002) distinguish usefully between "children's services" (provided, like formal playgrounds in cities, for children by adults) and "children's spaces" (the set of urban spaces, cultural, physical and social, in which children engage with adults and others as part of the city). Under the Italian Child Friendly City framework, local planning authorities have autonomy in interpreting this matter. Sometimes, their efforts have encouraged children to explore the city, rather than limiting them to formal playgrounds separate from it. In one instance, "play-buses" have transported groups of children to a certain city street, closing it off to traffic temporarily, and encouraging children to play in that unfamiliar setting (UNICEF 2005, 29). Children, as urban citizens, experience the joys of discovering a new part of the city, home to strangers, but only disrupting it temporarily by their presence.

A third example is the making of new contacts in the informality of a community center. Informality and home-like interiors characterize many urban community centers—be they drop-in centers attracting people with few resources, or neighborhood houses visited weekly by new immigrants in a suburb to engage in classes to improve their skills in the local language. Convivial relationships can be established between visitors and staff, and sometimes friendships between visitors themselves. One of the important issues emerging in the management of these centers is whether their informality should be reduced, their social environments more "managed." Governments find it hard to resist placing referral services for social service programs or adult education classes in centers whose informality is what has created there an environment of conviviality, of homeliness. Then there is the wish to hold the centers accountable for the "success" with which they have delivered these services. We agree with Conradson, who takes the strong view that centers offering people the opportunity merely to relate to each other, casually over a cup of tea in the kitchen or in activities they choose to enroll in, should not be assessed for funding by their success in offering formal programs (Conradson 2003, 521).

Libraries, streets, and community centers, then, can be the fertile ground in which convivial encounters take root. Notably, such spaces have involved planning. But this is not the kind of controlling planning of which the likes of Leonie Sandercock (2003) have been so critical. Rather, as Lisa Peattie has argued:

> Conviviality can take place with few props: the corner out of the wind where friends drink coffee together, the vacant lot which will become a garden. … Conviviality cannot be coerced, but it can be encouraged by the right rules, the right props, and the right places and spaces. (Peattie 1998, 248).

Important in this beguiling comment is the sentiment that conviviality, those important, often-casual and informal interactions, cannot be forced or coerced: convivial encounters are the product of planning with a "light touch," organizing without requiring compliance to set outcomes. Here, we particularly like the way Peattie's approach focuses our attention on both the micro-scale places in which encounters may take place, and the metropolitan scale through which services such as libraries, playbuses and community centers are funded and provided.

Figure 1. An encounter at a food co-operative. Photograph by Kate Shaw.

We see these convivial encounters as examples of the kind of ethical practices which are one (although by no means the only) characteristic of everyday life in cities. This is a kind of being together that is not reducible to shared identities—rather, it is a practice of temporary identification with others in a shared space. To make these connections with others is to cultivate the life of the city. As such, we think that excavating the practice and possibility of conviviality in cities can suggest strategies for repair and renewal, especially if we extend the principle of conviviality to all of the others with whom we share the city, human and non-human.

5: Risking Attachment in the Anthropocene

Lesley Instone

The notion of risk is now commonplace. For Ulrich Beck (1992) who introduced the term "risk society" in the early 1990s, contemporary ecological crises are not questions about the destruction of nature, but rather ones of how modern society deals with self-generated uncertainties that are no longer limited by time or space. These are dangers that escape and elide risk, calculation and insurability. In the face of permanent material threats, Beck argues that modern industrial society normalizes risk, and we become blind to side effects and consequences. Most of the time those of us in developed countries carry on our daily lives as if everything is insurable, as if we're neither causing environmental damage nor being affected by it, a sort of amnesia to the wider implications of ordinary action. For example, where I live, the mining and export of coal is a commonplace and everyday activity. Despite the challenges of climate change, coal trains deposit their loads, in ever increasing quantities, to the port of Newcastle (Australia) to be exported to power stations in China and elsewhere. The ethics of "deplete, destroy, depart" (Grinde and Johansen 1995 in Weir 2009, 119) go on in a way that becomes ordinary, everyday and unremarkable, and the dangers of dust, environmental degradation and climate change, are in Beck's terms, normalized.

Figure 1. Coal Trains, Newcastle, Australia. Photograph by Lesley Instone.

Inherent in Beck's notion of the risk society are the impulses of denial and surprise. Beck contends that in modern technological society risks are opaque—we can't easily see or identify them without the aid of scientific experts to help reveal the facts of the matter. This opaqueness leads to surprise when apparently benign things—certain foods or everyday activities, for example—turn out to be a risk to health and wellbeing. So, in the face of risk, we turn to the twin compensations of calculability and certainty. The irony of risk, says Beck (2006), is that the more we attempt control, the more likely we'll be surprised by the very things we think we're managing. Beck's analysis suggests that when faced with the "gargantuan agency and an almost unbearable level of responsibility" that the Anthropocene heralds (Gibson-Graham and Roelvink 2010, 2), we're likely to react with numbness, disconnection and resentment.

The disabling dynamics of risk as danger seem pervasive, but science studies scholar Bruno Latour suggests another prospect. Rather than reducing risk or insuring ourselves against it, Latour (2004a) suggests we focus on cultivating relations that embrace the possibilities that risk affords. This is how I understand Latour's notion of "risky attachments". For Latour, "risk-free objects, the smooth objects to which we had been accustomed up to now," the "matters of fact" of insurability and control in Beck's terms, "are giving way to *risky attachments*, tangled objects" (2004a, 22, italics in original). Risky attachments are not so much about danger, but about possibility; the possibilities that emerge from acknowledging our entanglements in and with things. There are no "side effects," externalization of dangers, risk free objects, or simple "matters of fact" for Latour, everything, he says, is tangled up in messy imbroglios that can't be reduced to constituent parts. So risky attachments, are "matters of concern," rather than "matters of fact", that gather up a mélange of humans, non-humans, technologies and the like in constituting the relations that compose the Anthropocene. This isn't to say that there are no dangers or problems, but to start from the idea that embracing our attachments and embeddedness in complex networks offers hope rather than menace. Such a stance means different ways of thinking and doing that connect us as one among the many actors and places that enact the world.

For example, the practice of risky attachment resonates with Jess Weir's (2009) shift of register from despair to repair. Weir suggests that the generative practices of engaging with loss (rather than denying it) can be a positive motivating force for renewal and repair. From her work with the Indigenous Yorta Yorta people along the Murray River, she calls for communicative relations between people and country that recognize the capacity of country to act, and the appreciation that country is alive and speaks for itself when people choose to listen. Likewise, Margaret Somerville points out that the dominant story of the Murray-Darling Basin as a system in distress and hopelessness, is only one among many possible stories. The dominant story positions the river as an object in need of intervention, as a problem of calculation that requires modes of control that insure against risk. But the Indigenous stories that Somerville works with suggest a different world of intimate attachment, of being present *with* the land (2009, 212–214, emphasis mine). This is a world of connections and flows where the embodied experience of place transforms the story of despair about the Murray-Darling Basin to a story of collective responsibility to "sing it back to life, together, all of us" (2009, 221), and a willingness to enact a shared postcolonial politics of place.

Postcolonial place is implicit in Val Plumwood's (2008) concept of shadow places. These denied places highlight the spatiality of risky attachments and the relations of detachment on which they are built. Plumwood argues that a harmful disconnection underpins consumer society, creating shadow places as sacrificed or denied spaces, "all those places that produce or are affected by the commodities you consume, places consumers don't know about, don't want to know about, and in a commodity regime don't ever need to know about or take responsibility for" (2008, 146–147). As risky attachments, shadow places are not places "out there," instead they're part of "our" place, not separate but intimately interlinked with who and where we are. When we risk attachment to shadow places, we enact a critical ecology of place recognizing the other not as danger, but as related.

Risky attachments cut across the modernist categories of nature and culture, they stretch out to make connections with unlike and unlikely others, they cross boundaries between humans and nonhumans, the organic and inorganic, and displace humans as the only actor. As a risky attachment, coal, for example, would no longer be imagined as an isolated mineral, but thickly embedded in complex networks of lives, lungs, climate, multinational corporations, government revenues, biodiversity, and the like. Imagine large lumps of coal polished to a high sheen, glistening and gorgeous, displayed on shelves or bejeweling a mini Ferris wheel. Such a transformation is part of Andrew Drummond's engagement with coal, that archetypal modern commodity whose risky attachments continue to bind 19th-century industrialism to the Anthropocene. From his converted powerhouse home, Drummond listens to the thundering of coal trains as they pass by, and ponders the meaning and potent energy of this ubiquitous mineral. His art probes the metaphorical power of coal and the complex relations between land, body and the transformative potential of the material.

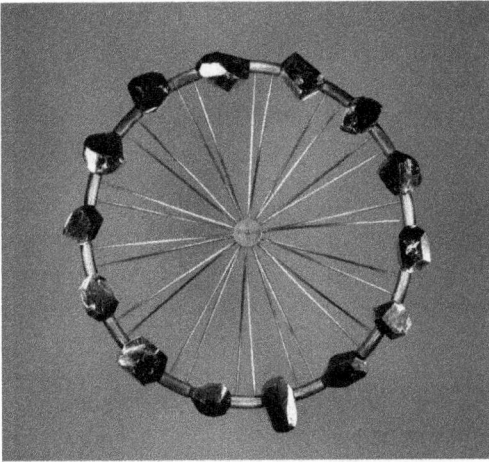

Figure 2. Coal Wheel. Andrew Drummond, 1997-98. Brass, coal, bearings 1600mm diameter x 300mm various. Collection of the artist. Photograph by John Collie.

Paradoxically, Drummond's shiny polished nuggets of coal could be stand-ins for Latour's smooth risk-free objects whose slippery surfaces eschew any attachments: coal as separate, singular, a matter of fact. But Drummond has crafted risky attachments of coal to land and bodies, to the rhythms of industry, and brought to life though kinetic sculptures a mundane but potent commodity. "It's one of those really banal things," he says, "things that people walk past and don't even see. I find that really fascinating" (Drummond in Blundell 2006). Drummond's installations enact the multiplicity of coal's agency in mines, in chemical reactions, and his kinetic works conjure alchemical potentials and shifting forms that link the bodies of miners, laboratory staff, engineers, and landscapes in webs of destruction and potential. As a "matter of concern" coal is intimately bound up in our lives and the lives of non-humans. Drummond's art reveals coal as an active element in us, outside us and alongside us and demonstrates the shift from coal as an inert object to coal as a risky and active entanglement. From the small everyday deposits of dust in lungs, depletion of biodiversity with mine expansion, to the multinational mining and shipping companies, and so on, coal is entangled in the distributed networks that unevenly knot together humans, nature and technology.

Risky attachments also stretch time. Musician and artist Brian Eno (2000) invokes a temporal dimension of risky attachments with his concept of "the long now." "'Now' is never just a moment," says Eno. "The Long Now is the recognition that the precise moment you're in grows out of the past and is the seed for the future. The longer your sense of Now, the more past and future it includes" (2000). Eno's "Long Now" risks the connection of past and future and the responsibility this implies for our actions in the present. To exemplify a new temporality of the Anthropocene, the Long Now Foundation is working on a 10,000-year clock that encompasses the principles of simplicity, going slow, expecting trouble and restarts, and easy reparability.[1] The "long now" percolates into the future and challenges us to think and act differently. As a risky attachment the 10,000-year clock generates new rhythms of time and new networks of risky thinking.

Risky thinking, in Isabel Stengers' terms, is to think possibility against probability; the transformation of risk to hope. Against the sort of insurability and calculation at the center of the "risk society," Stengers advocates an "experimental stance, an adventure in life": the risk of possibility, the risk of

---

[1] The Long Now Foundation, http://www.longnow.org/clock/.

"laughter and joy in the face of uncertainty" (quoted in Zournazi 2002, 244). Life, for Stengers, isn't built upon certainty and insurances, "but upon the situation or events that make them possible" (quoted in Zournazi 2002, 244), and it is in the interstices of encounter that, for her, hope is to be found. Stengers insists that risk is not an abstraction, not a romantic gesture of "risking everything," nor something that can be done on behalf of others. Instead, for Stengers, risk is a concrete experience that slows us down enough to take time, value experience and hold onto hope and joy. So, in Stengers' terms "risky attachments" are events, they're active relations of hope and connection in which we cannot predict the outcomes, where we risk opening ourselves to possibility, and risk letting our thinking spill out beyond our questions and theories. In the act, she insists, we risk ourselves, and the possibility of putting our own ideas at risk in the "hope that something could be produced" (quoted in Zournazi 2002, 248). From this perspective, it's not the risk of danger that is central but the risk of hope, of feeling and thinking, that in Stengers' words, "oblige me to think and feel in a new way" and that induce "the powerful sense that something else is possible" (quoted in Zournazi 2002, 246, 248).

Writing this from my home next to the coal loader in the world's largest coal port, it's easy to feel the inducement of despair and disconnection, to rigidify thinking, to favor control against hope, to disregard the shadow places up the valley being devastated by open cut mining, and to ignore those shadow places in Asia overwhelmed by pollution from burning coal. We're all too familiar with disconnectedness as a practiced strategy. But things are shifting, people are making connections, they're thinking beyond the limits of a blinkered "now." For example, ex-coal miner Graham Brown now campaigns against coal expansion, saying that many in the industry are "interested in where they fit into the situation" (Manning 2009). Another, a fifth generation coal miner, anonymously tells a journalist that he's anxious that pits may have to close, but, he confides, "there is no life on a dead planet" (Eastley 2009).

For me, an ethics for the Anthropocene calls for an ecology of risky attachments. The shift to recognizing our entanglements in the imbroglios of the Anthropocene—biodiversity loss, global warming, social injustice—is an important first step. But more than this, is the act of *risking* attachment, the active search for different and interconnected practices of feeling, thought, and action. Paradoxically the dangers and risks that the Anthropocene heralds may be best addressed not with insurance and control, but through reaching out and risking attachment with all manner of unlike others. In risking attachment we risk our thoughts and feelings, and plunge ourselves into a world of matters of concern; a complex, hybrid and multi-species world where uncertainty reigns. Latour, Stengers, and others remind us that feeling and thinking are mutually constituted, and that assembling tangled objects and risking attachment are generative events "whose outcome cannot be anticipated" (Stengers, quoted in Zournazi 2002, 265). To meet the challenges of the Anthropocene, scientist Will Steffen (2009) argues that the "future will depend on the nature of human aspirations, values, preferences and choices … nothing less than a transformation is needed." Such a transformation will not be abstract or grand, it will be multiple, ordinary and everyday, forged in the unfinished and hopeful work of risking attachment.

6: *STRATEGIA*
THINKING WITH OR ACCOMMODATING THE WORLD

FREYA MATHEWS

If we want to escape the grip of the dualistic categories that have disenchanted and de-animated our world in the Western tradition, and thereby rendered it a fit object for domination and control, we may require something more than a purely discursive or *theoretical* approach to reality. We may require a mode of cognition that is cultivated not merely through abstract "reflection" but through practice—specific forms of *strategic* practice.

It was a brilliant and arresting article by Francois Jullien (2002), "Did Philosophers Have to Become Fixated on Truth?" that first alerted me to the possible contingency of truth as the goal of cognition. And it was the meta-level contrast Jullien drew between the figure of the Greek philosopher and that of the Chinese sage that somehow made this contingency of truth as a goal plain. Jullien observes that the sage set out not to explain the world, as the philosopher did, but to adapt or accommodate himself to it. The sage sought to identify the tendencies or dispositions at work in particular situations in order to harness those tendencies or dispositions to his own best advantage. To this end he remained open to all points of view instead of insisting, as philosophers did, on a single viewpoint ("truth") exclusive of others. In describing the sage as seeking "congruence" with reality, Jullien seems to be implying that the thinking of the sage remained inextricable from agency rather than becoming, like the thinking of the Greeks, an end in itself.

This contrast between the Greek philosopher and the Chinese sage might be further elaborated via the above-mentioned contrast between theory and strategy. Theorists focus on the world as representation, a completed abstract totality projected by the subject onto a cognitive screen; understood as such a totality, the world is then perceived as external to and independent of the subject. Strategists focus rather on the immediate field of influences in which they are immersed and the way in which that field impacts upon their agency. That is, as strategists we are concerned not with an idealized "world," conceived under its universal aspect, but rather with our own immediate situation and how the influences at play in it are impinging on us, corporeally and tangibly, in the present moment. Our focus shifts from world as ideal double or mirrored image, to world as immediate field of active influences in which we are agentically immersed. We do not need a theory about the nature of reality in order to respond strategically to this field: we feel environmental pressures increasing and decreasing as we respond now this way, now that. There is no sense of this world as a completed totality; it extends just as far as the range of our own sensitivity, and as we move around in it this range is constantly changing. To train the strategic faculty, one does not teach reason, which is to say, the rules of logic and abstraction, but rather one sets exercises or practices which cultivate sensitivity and responsiveness. This is why Chinese sages typically received their training in martial and other Daoist arts rather than in discursive inquiry.

Strategic consciousness then, unlike discursive consciousness, is inherently non-dualist, not because it is unself-consciousness, but because it doesn't project "a world" into an abstract space of re-presentation beyond the agency of the self, where it can be grasped as a bounded totality. Rather, the strategic self remains immersed in a fluxing field of immediate pressures which are registered not "objectively," as part of a totality at an epistemic remove from the subject, but in terms of their immediate impact or influence on the agency of the self. Etymology is helpful here. "Theory" is derived from the Greek *theoria*, a looking at, thing looked at; *theoros*, spectator; and *thea*, spectacle. "Strategy" is derived from the Greek *strategia*, "office or command or art of a general," from *stratos*, "multitude, army, expedition" and *agein*, "to lead, guide, drive, carry off," from Sanskrit *ajirah*, "moving, active." In light of this, strategy may be understood as concerned with the coordination of collective or individual agency. Cognition is required for such coodination, but this is not the kind of cognition involved in *theoria*, which abstracts from the empirical agency of the subject in order to attain a more "objective" rendering of the world. In *strategia*, cognition remains in the service of agency.

However—and this is an important point—it is not as though the sage, by staking out his epistemological standpoint within the terrain of his own agency and cultivating sensitivity to the immediate and particular influences impinging on him, does not discover anything about the nature of reality. What he discovers is that *strategia* does indeed call for accommodation. The best way of negotiating the field of influences in which one is immersed—where this field includes the cross-cutting wills or conativities of others—is generally to adapt to them. That is to say, the best way of negotiating this field is to make one's own ends as consistent as possible with those influences and conativities, rather than seeking to force them into compliance with one's own will. This is self-evident in as much as he who achieves his goals in ways best calculated to conserve his own energy will be most fit to continue to preserve and increase his own existence. *Strategia* then points to *wu wei*, the way of least resistance, which can be understood not simply as the giving up of one's own ends in deference to the ends of others but rather as tailoring one's ends to those already in train in one's environment, and using the energies already at play in that environment to further one's goals.

Today it is of course the scientist who is the great descendent of the Greek philosopher with his theoretical orientation to reality. Our Western approach to environmental crisis accordingly follows this scientific suit. We seek to understand nature in scientific terms then manipulate and manage it in accordance with those terms, bringing it back into conformity with our current theoretical—for example, ecological—ideals. But such *management* of nature clearly perpetuates the attitude that led to our environmental troubles in the first place. It was treating nature as an external object that could first be re-presented in theoretical terms then manipulated in accordance with prescribed ends that launched us on the path of environmental domination and control that has brought us into the ecological meltdown of the Anthropocene.

Figure 1. Laozi, prophet of *wu wei*, rides west towards immortality. Painting on the wall of a ruined temple in the Wudang Mountains. Photograph by Freya Mathews.

The figure of the sage, beckoning us down the path of *wu wei* (see *fig. 1*), perhaps offers a new point of departure outside the compromised parameters of environmental management. *Wu wei* points not so much towards remedial environmentalism as towards a new approach to crafting our civilization, a new stance of accommodation in the shaping of all our systems. In accordance with *wu wei*, these systems would henceforth be devised *with* the grain of in situ conativities rather than in accordance with preconceived designs. Food production would respond to and nourish local ecologies rather than rendering land a *tabula rasa* for industrial monoculture. Manufacture would follow the circular, no-waste model that returns all resource materials back into the loop of production. Architecture and engineering would follow the contours of local topography and make full use of local affordances with respect to materials, energy, ventilation, water capture, cycling and dispersal (Mathews 2011b). Even economics and politics could be conducted on *wu wei* lines, where this would involve a decentralized approach, the nurturing, again, of local affordances: local knowledge and culture, local talent and intelligence, local initiative and responsibility as well as local physical resources.

A beautiful example of a hydro-engineering scheme explicitly designed in accordance with the principle of *wu wei* is the ancient irrigation system of Dujiangyan, established in 256 BCE on the Min River in the Chinese province of Sichuan. The system was built to protect local people from the dangerous annual flooding of the river. Instead of constructing a dam, the then governor, Li Bing, devised a series of channels, held in place by bamboo baskets filled with stones, that harmlessly and productively dispersed the flood waters across the flood plain, making that flood plain the richest agricultural area in China. In contrast to the massive dams that have been an unfortunate hallmark of China's development in the latter half of the twentieth century, the Dujiangyan system does not damage the ecology of the river, even though it reconfigures it: fish and other aquatic life have free passage through the system. Whereas dams generally succumb to ecological death and silt-up in a matter of decades, and are thought to contribute to geological instability, Dujiangyan is still as benignly functional and productive today as it was more than two thousand years ago, and it emerged almost unscathed from the catastrophic Sichuan earthquake of 2008 (Watts 2010).

What I am here calling the strategic approach is then far from new, and even in the West many of the design principles that conform to it are already staples of sustainability thinking, falling under the rubric of biomimicry, for instance. But to figure this approach as strategic is to recognize its origins in a deeply counter-Western, and hence counter-dualist, mindset, that should protect us, if we remain mindful of it, from unconsciously reproducing, in our environmental thinking, the attitudes at the root of environmental abuse.

7: CONTACT IMPROVISATION
DANCE WITH THE EARTH BODY YOU HAVE

KATE RIGBY

Contact Improvisation is a form of dance. As the name suggests, this is not the kind of dance where everybody knows the steps in advance. While its moves are unscripted, Contact Improvisation also differs from the semi-solo style of arm-flailing and hip-swiveling in which many of us learnt to engage as teenagers, for its practitioners are required to remain at all times in close proximity to a partner. "Characteristically performed in a duet," explains Hellene Gronda:

> Contact Improvisation combines the freedom to move spontaneously with an injunction to maintain a physical relationship with your partner(s), usually through touch, but also through commitment to a mutual trajectory based on a shared centre of gravity. Body awareness is fundamental to safe practice of the form because it is likely to include falling and spatial disorientation. It can be awkward, spectacularly dangerous, or breathtaking and tender. ... Contact Improvisation is primarily practiced in a community activity called a Jam. (Gronda 2005, 28–29)

Although the moves of this dance are unrehearsed and

unpredictable, often requiring "reactions much faster than conscious calculation" (Gronda 2005, 14), the skills required to do it well—and no one can do it perfectly—are developed through rigorous training and disciplined practice. Above all, to practice Contact Improvisation with some degree of safety, it is essential that you pay close attention to your own body, as much as that of your partner, learning to "dance with the body you have" by familiarizing yourself with its capacities and constraints, its tendencies and resistances, and attuning yourself constantly to where it is taking you in your volatile corporeal communion with one or more others.

In her remarkable doctoral thesis on Contact Improvisation, Gronda ponders how the practice of dancing with the body you have engenders a relational and deconstructive subjectivity, in which selfhood is experienced as neither separable from, nor reducible to, the body that I have no alternative but to take as "mine," one that is at once "a part of the physical world that can be acted upon, and the part of the physical world that enables me to act" (Gronda 2005, 16); a body, sometimes agreeable but not infrequently pesky, that turns out to have its own relatively autonomous agency, while remaining ineluctably embedded in a multi-facetted socio-ecological continuum, that is itself both delimiting and enabling. Neither the sum total of what I am, nor a mere means to my conscious ends, this is a body that "can be listened to, engaged in dialogue, trusted, witnessed and befriended" (Gronda 2005, 32).

As Gronda observes, entering into a respectfully dialogic relationship with that "little bit of nature I call my own," while noticing also how it is scored by the social (for this "little bit" is no more purely "natural" than the wider physical environment in which it is embedded), provides a possible opening onto a decentered, non-dualistic way of relating to materiality in general. Indeed, Contact Improvisation was said by Steve Paxton, its originator in New York in the 1970s, to have begun with "a state of trust of the body *and the earth*" (Paxton 1982, 17, emphasis mine). In this essay, I want to explore further the eco-philosophical implications of Contact

Improvisation, by considering what it might mean to dance with the "earth body" that we have.

"Earth body" might be taken to signify my own body, understood as a thing of Earth, as is that of all creatures, human and otherwise, with whom I share an earthly existence in the "dance" of life; alternatively, it could refer to Earth itself, understood as a matrix of geological, hydrological, atmospheric and biological entities and processes, the greater "body" within which my small human one attains, temporarily, its own quasi-autonomous existence. Focusing, as I wish to do here, on this second referent, the call to "dance with the earth body you have" invokes what is, at least for now, an impossible possibility: namely, that we could inhabit, and hence "dance with," a planet other than this one.

Within Eurowestern modernity, it is possible to discern a tendency to act precisely as if we did, or could, do this. For instance, we have acted as if Earth were such that it would continue indefinitely to satisfy the insatiable demands that we continue to place upon it; and as it has become apparent that this would not be the case, we have turned our attention with new zeal to the space-age project of inter-planetary imperialism (as extension of the "logic of colonization" [Plumwood 1993] that previously brought terrestrial "new worlds" under European rule). Other forms of Earth denial preceded this, of course, and persist in some quarters today: notably, in those religious and philosophical systems, Western and otherwise, that locate our true existence in an otherworldly elsewhere that can be fully entered into only by throwing off our earthbound "mortal coil." The techno-utopian counterpart to such dreams of spiritual transcendence manifests in another form of Earth denial, oriented towards the wholesale transformation of the planet with a view to rendering it more docile and subservient to human interests (another colonizing tendency that is also evident in the treatment of our own bodies, no longer simply as a surface for make-up, but as a target for intrusive make-over). Carolyn Merchant views this as a secularized version of the Christian narrative of "paradise regained," and she argues that there is also an environmentalist version of the "recovery plot" in the quest to re-store what is mistakenly believed to have been a prior condition of ecological harmony and stability (Merchant 1995, 27–56): mistaken, that is, in light of contemporary understandings of dynamic change and discord as a natural feature of Earth's inherently unstable ecology (Botkin 1992).

Figure 1. Cyclone Yasi. Source: Google maps.

To not merely inhabit, but to "dance with" the earth body you have is to live your earthly life more intensely, ethically and potentially also more joyously, recognizing constraints but also extending your capacities in and through your relations with those whom you partner in the dance, and alongside whom you "jam." This begins with fully embracing an Earthian identity, accepting that right now it is this planet, and no other, that is your home, and more than that: it is flesh of your flesh, bone of your bone. It is also means acknowledging that Earth, along with the myriad earth bodies, such as yourself, human and otherwise, that live as quasi-autonomous beings within it, has its own interests and agency that demand to be respected. Earth is both a part of the physical world that can be acted upon by humans, and the part of the physical world that enables us to act as corporeal beings: we should therefore do our best, within the limits of our power and knowledge, to ensure that the ways in which we act upon it do not damage its capacity to enable us, and other earth beings, to continue to act, and, ideally, dance with it and one another, in the future. And if we are to practice this dance well, if inevitably imperfectly, we will have to treat Earth as a body that can be listened to, engaged in dialogue, trusted, witnessed and befriended. By familiarizing ourselves with its capacities and constraints, its tendencies and resistances, we become better attuned to where we are heading in our volatile corporeal interactions with those with whom we are jamming (see *figs. 1 & 2*). And if, perchance, we are heading for a fall, this will hopefully improve our chances of minimizing the potential harm to ourselves and our partners, human and otherwise, as we go down.

Figure 2. A man flees the Category 5 Cyclone Yasi at the Esplanade, Cairns, February 2011. Picture by Patrick Hamilton. Source: *The Australian.*

In today's world especially, dancing with the earth body we have entails reckoning with a "dark ecology" (Morton 2007): the reality of widespread and ramifying damage, largely of human making, and the likelihood of increasingly uncongenial alterations to come. For most people, most of the time, earthly existence has never been easy: little wonder that dreams of escape or mastery have proven so attractive (if by no means universally so). However, the increasing climatic variability, reduced predictability and more frequent and intense extremes wrought by global warming, even should we succeed in mitigating it to some degree, suggests that learning to dance with the earth body we have has become considerably trickier, as well as more necessary, than ever before. Honing our skills of environmental contact improvisation (Rigby 2009), such as those that survive in some Indigenous cultures to this day, including among the exceptionally weather-wise of Australia (Rose 2005), might give us the best chance we have, if not to preserve the socio-ecological status quo, then at least to reduce the damage should it fall.

Stories Shared

8: VULTURE STORIES
NARRATIVE AND CONSERVATION

THOM VAN DOOREN

Vultures are never very far from death, never very far from the carcasses that they strip bare so cleanly and efficiently. Like all of Earth's scavengers, they play a vital role in transforming waste and putrefaction into nourishment, creating a safer environment for so many other living things. Change and transformation are at the heart of their place in more-than-human communities—death becomes life again. And so, death is not a bad thing in any simple way: inside tangled processes of multi-species becoming, everyone is food for someone else, and nobody, no species, lives forever. And yet, in some cases we want to reject death, we want to say that there has been too much of it, or it has come too soon—again, both in the case of individuals and of species. This is a story about the vultures of India, but it is also an attempt to think through *why* one might tell stories in a time of extinction, what it might mean to make a storied stand for some deaths and not others.

In conversations about vultures in India, people have often recounted to me having seen large numbers of these birds gathered along the banks of rivers consuming the dead bodies of cattle and other animals, including sometimes people, as they float by or wash up on the water's edge. When it meets a vultures' beak it matters very little if this flesh was once a human or some other kind of animal. While people have long been meals for vultures all over the world, in India it is domestic cattle that have traditionally comprised most of their meals (van Dooren 2011a). This situation has in the past worked out very well for both people and vultures, but in recent decades it has become the cause of untold harm for both groups, as well as numerous other species.

While vultures in India certainly benefited from the fact that it is one of the most cattle rich countries in the world, from a vulture's perspective what has made India an ideal place to live is the fact that most of the cows there are not consumed by people. Hindu reverence for cattle, alongside a more general ethos of *ahimsa* (or nonviolence towards all living things), has produced a complex cultural and religious environment in which most Indians do not eat beef, and many are vegetarian (Robbins 1998).

When they die, cows are usually either taken to carcass dumps or left at the edge of villages, often after being skinned for leather. By and large it is vultures that have been relied upon in India to "take care" of these bodies—an estimated five to ten million cow, camel and buffalo carcasses each year (McGrath 2007). In this context, vultures often lived quite closely with human communities. In urban and semi-urban environments, they found abundant food in carcass dumps, as well as in tanneries, slaughter yards, garbage dumps, and bone mills. And it was not just vultures that benefited from this association. These industries, and local communities, were provided with a free and efficient means of carcass disposal for the millions of cows that they kept but did not eat (as well as the waste products from numerous other kinds of animals).

But now these vultures are dying. In recent decades the vultures of India and the surrounding region have been poisoned en masse by diclofenac, an anti-inflammatory drug given to many of the cattle whose carcasses they then consume. In a vulture's body, this drug causes painful swelling, inflammation, and eventually kidney failure and death. Over roughly the past two decades, around 95 percent of India's vultures are thought to have died in this way (Pain et al. 2008).

In the emergence of vulture-toxic cattle, we encounter the flip side of the proximity and entanglement between people and vultures discussed above. While their close association has for a long time been mutually advantageous, it has now become a liability for everyone. Domesticated cattle once provided a great source of carrion for vultures, but this reliance on humans (more accurately on livestock that they keep) may now lead to vultures' extinction.

Similarly, the entanglement and close proximity of people and vultures in India has become a liability for human communities. In their absence, it has been made all too clear how important a role vultures played, through the consumption of the dead, in creating an environment in which so much other life could flourish. In particular, it is now feared by many scientists that unscavenged cattle carcasses may cause an increase in the populations of fast breeding scavengers like rats and street dogs, who could in turn spread diseases like rabies. India is already home to 60 percent of the world's rabies deaths—approximately 25 to 30,000 people die of this disease each year, primarily contracted through dog bites. The vast majority of these people are from lower socioeconomic groups (APCRI 2004). But these diseases don't just have the potential to harm people: in addition to the awful deaths suffered by dogs with rabies, increased dog populations might also spread rabies and other diseases like canine distemper virus and canine parvovirus to livestock, and even other animals like hyenas, jackals, tigers and Asiatic lions— some of whom are "members" of critically endangered species themselves (van Dooren 2010).

In addition to the spread of disease, the disappearance of vultures has given rise to important economic and cultural consequences for some. Bone collectors, who sell cattle bones to the fertiliser industry may now have to clean the bones themselves, while the Parsi community—who have traditionally exposed their dead to vultures in a process called *dokhmenishini*—have faced a range of difficulties in figuring out how to take care of the dead in a world without vultures (Markandya et al. 2008; Swan et al. 2006; van Dooren 2011a).

This very short vulture story highlights some of the important roles that narrative might play in conservation work. Narratives allow us to weave diverse materials—scientific research, ethnography, history and philosophy, amongst others—into a single account. Whilst necessarily partial and incomplete, these stories nevertheless allow us to develop "thick" accounts of the species that we are describing; that is, accounts that draw in diverse voices in a way that might enable an audience to develop a sense of curiosity about them and concern for their futures. As James Hatley (2000) has argued so eloquently in another context, unlike a mere recitation of the "facts," narrative is often able to expose its audience to the struggles and suffering of others in a way that makes a demand upon them for response and responsibility.

But this "thick" account is not simply of an organism or a species in isolation. Narrative also plays a vital role in holding together the complexity and tangled connections that are more-than-human ecologies. In Tom Griffiths' (2007) words, narrative "enacts connectivity." As in the vulture story I have just told, this connectivity works across nature/culture, human/non-human, ecology/economy, life/death boundaries—it entangles humans within extinction stories in a range of different ways (Rose and van Dooren 2011).

But for all this complexity, the story that I have told is still remarkably simple, perhaps *too* simple. The bare bones of the causal chain that I have outlined—from diclofenac poisoning to carcasses piling up, increased dog numbers and rabies deaths—has been popular with many conservation biologists and journalists. I suspect that the story is mostly accurate, but there are considerable holes in the evidence for parts of it. In many ways this simplification of conservation narratives is an essential part of their power. Simple causal stories—especially ones that start with single causes, like diclofenac—are important for conservation agendas precisely because they provide (relatively) simple explanations and avenues for action. In many cases, these stories do vital work in generating public and government awareness, concern and response, as well as in all important fundraising work (which, amongst other things, is necessary to conduct the research that will fill gaps in the evidence). As humanities scholars telling conservation stories, we are often required to walk the thin line between two very political necessities: bringing in otherwise unheard voices, helping to make new connections across assumed divides (in short introducing complexity), while on the other hand not unnecessarily complicating a scientific narrative that may have real conservation efficacy.

Telling situated stories, stories that also think about the means and consequences of their own telling, is vitally important here. These are the stories that we need for the Anthropocene, stories that take the complexity of *change,* and draw in some of the myriad beings—human and not—for whom this change is all too often experienced as suffering and loss. And so these must also be stories that ask their audiences to be curious and to care about the many relationships, the many ways of being, the many worlds that are disappearing in bright bursts of pain in this time of escalating extinctions.

Figure 1. Critically endangered Indian vulture (*Gyps bengalensis*). Photograph by Lip Kee. This photograph is reproduced under a CC BY-SA 2.0 license.

9: Learning to be Affected by Earth Others

Gerda Roelvink

If, as Val Plumwood (2002) suggests, we can no longer be-
have as isolated and masterful human individuals, nations or
species, but need to act in accordance with those earth others
enabling our existence, what does this mean for the activity
of research? One answer might be to seek out those who are
already transforming their relationships with the more than
human world, to learn about and tell their stories, and to help
multiply, magnify, legitimate and proliferate their practices.
If one looks for them, there are many who are engaged in
learning from our climate changed earth in such a way that
they themselves are transformed and are prompted to create
new ways of living with earth others. Bruno Latour (2004b)
calls this process that co-transforms the learner and the
world "learning to be affected." Central to learning to be affected is a process whereby one becomes sensitized to (affected by) a world that in turn becomes more highly differentiated (see Latour 2004b; Gibson-Graham and Roelvink 2010).
In this essay I want to tentatively suggest that by connecting
with those already affected by the manifestations of climate
change academic researchers too might learn to be affected.

Australian farmers have long been engaged in modes of
learning that aim to increase their store of scientific
knowledge and promote more efficient farming practices.

Agricultural research and extension involves farmers in participatory learning with experts and practitioners exchanging knowledge within established agricultural science paradigms. But rarely do we hear of farmers who, by observing and listening to the land and by empathizing with plants and animals, are driven to go against the prevailing scientific wisdom and farm in new ecologically sensitive ways. John Weatherstone and Peter Andrews are two such farmers. Central to their radical shifts in agricultural practice has been their affective experience of the Anthropocene, in particular their witness to ecological devastation (Roelvink and Zolkos 2011).

John Weatherstone (2003) recalls the "day from hell" when he went out to survey his land as a dust storm blew away the remaining fertile topsoil (see *fig. 1*). By embracing this moment of devastation, Weatherstone was able to notice that while the wind was blowing fertile topsoil off his farm the neglected and weedy nature strip along the highway that borders his property was able to retain soil. That is, he became attuned to the diversity of grasses on his farm. He identifies this as the moment he decided, "I'm going to do everything in my power to see that this farm never looks like this again" (Weatherstone 2010, personal communication). At an early age farmer Peter Andrews was similarly affected by witnessing the devastation of his father's outback farm. Watching the dust storms he realized that, "without the scrub that had always protected it, the land was exposed to the weather. The winds could now rip and tear at the earth. It was my first lesson in how, within a decade or two, people could drastically affect a landscape that had been operating successfully for tens of thousands of years" (Andrews 2006, 16). The motivation for both farmers to transform their farms is intimately linked with their relationships to other species and the landscape in a changing environment. Importantly, the new farming practices developed by Peter Andrews and John Weatherstone are guided by a recognition of the needs of the environment and animals, and working with the capacities of earth others for resilience (Rose 2004).

Figure 1. John Weatherstone's farm on Christmas Eve 1982. Photograph courtesy of Weatherstone.[1]

Andrews' and Weatherstone's (2003) stories demonstrate the radically transformative practices that can be generated through learning to be affected. After his experience of the day from hell Weatherstone went on to experiment on his farm by diversifying agricultural practices. He reduced livestock, planted a variety of trees, improved pastures and reduced chemical use. Rather than choosing trees on the sole basis of efficiency and profitability, he has planted trees that attract birds, provide shade and fodder for cows and provide for his own need for seeds to generate an income. Likewise, Weatherstone ensures that the soil has the organic matter it needs to survive through "the creation of smaller paddocks and the use of perennial pastures, rotational grazing, reducing cropping, and no stubble burning" (8). In doing so Weatherstone is taking other species into account in his livelihood decisions, thereby ensuring that his agricultural practices meet both his own needs for survival and those of the landscape and other species. Today his farm looks like an

[1] Previously published in Weatherstone 2003, 5.

oasis in a landscape of bare pastoral land and native birds that have not been seen in the area for decades have returned to Weatherstone's farm.

While Weatherstone has taken an experimental approach on this farm, Peter Andrews has conducted historical geographical research into the Australian landscape, giving particular attention to records of natural systems existing prior to European colonization (see Andrews 2006). Through his research, Andrews discovered that while the journals of early European explorers "are filled with descriptions of swamps and marshes . . . today ninety per cent of wetlands have disappeared" (6). Comparing these historical descriptions to the state of his property, he became increasingly concerned by the way that water was channeled through deep stream incisions, creating erosion and salinity problems and reducing nutrients. This research has led Andrews to develop Natural Sequence Farming, an innovative approach to farming that slows water flows across land to increase water retention (2006).

Figure 2. Cows grazing under a honey locust plantation on John Weatherstone's property. Photograph courtesy of Weatherstone.[2]

[2] Previously published in Weatherstone 2003, 10.

The new farming practices arising from John Weather-stone's and Peter Andrews' experimentation and historical geographical research were radical and initially left them iso-lated from the agricultural community. For example, a cattle carrier picking up stock from John Weatherstone comment-ed that "I used to drive past John Weatherstone's place regu-larly, and when he first started planting all the trees I thought he had rocks in his head. I now know it was me who had rocks in my head for not planting trees" (Weatherstone 2003, 7–8). After many years of neglect, the practices of farmers like Andrews and Weatherstone have attracted the attention of other famers and scientists. Academic researchers have begun to theorize and value what these farmers are doing. There is growing interest in diversifying the range of agricul-ture possibilities and moving away from over-specialization and monoculture. Some scientists are helping to shift the unorthodox farming practices of Andrews and Weatherstone from "cult status" into the mainstream. How have these aca-demic researchers connected to these innovative farmers and might they provide lessons for researchers more generally?

Land ecologist David Goldney, who travelled with a group of bureaucrats to meet Peter Andrews, remembers that they:

> laughed about Peter all the way there and … derided him all the way back … . But I saw something there that just kept drawing me back. And then I had to try and fit this stuff in to my existing scientific understanding. That took me ten years to do it. Now I think we can explain the pro-cess, you know in half an hour or less, ten minutes given the right sort of video help. (Goldney 2005)

There was something about Andrews' farm that kept drawing Goldney back until he could understand what An-drews was doing. It seems that Goldney was deeply affected by his experience of Andrews' farm; that is, by his experience of seeing farmers connecting in a new way with earth others and by bearing witness to the resilience and capacities for action of these new 'farmer-earth other' collectives. These stories suggest that we, as academic researchers, might look to such collectives of humans and earth others that are already learning to be affected in the Anthropocene. We might then join with them and work to proliferate the practices they are initiating.

These stories also demonstrate, I think, that one does not necessarily need to visit these farms to be affected and moved to transform one's research agenda (Gibson-Graham and Roelvink 2010). As testimony to their experience of ecological devastation, John Weatherstone's, Peter Andrews' and other stories in this volume call on us, the audience, to take their experiences seriously. The testimonial nature of these stories is important because it conveys an experience as it was lived and embodied rather than aiming to moralize or educate the audience in the value of a particular kind of agricultural practice (Roelvink and Zolkos 2011). This means that as recipients of their testimony we are offered possibilities to be affected by them in a profoundly personal way, in such a way that we too become implicated in these stories (Roelvink 2010). What they highlight, then, is the role that storytelling can have in linking us with those who are creating new ways of living in the Anthropocene.

10: THE WATERHOLE PROJECT
LOCATING RESILIENCE

GEORGE MAIN

The National Museum of Australia in Canberra records and interprets Australian social, Aboriginal and environmental history. As a curator and environmental historian employed by the Museum, my role is to foster understandings of human lives within the contexts of dynamic ecological systems. The National Museum is responsible for making sense of interactions between people and the rest of nature, and has a significant role to play in helping Australians grapple with the meanings of the profound climatic and ecological changes that define our time, the Anthropocene.

What historically and culturally determined ways of thinking and acting have generated anthropogenic climate change? What habits of thought and perception continue to block effective responses? Might we locate hopeful ways of thinking and acting to build social and ecological resilience as we enter an uncertain and difficult future? What understandings and possibilities emerge if we turn towards the local and to the material? These questions underlay The Waterhole Project, a research initiative that explores the meanings of climate change in relation to the ecological and social realities of a particular place called Combaning.

Figure 1. Combaning Creek waterhole, October 2010. Photograph
by George Main.

Combaning is a productive farming and pastoral district
about 300 kilometers southwest of Sydney, Australia. Through
the district weaves Combaning Creek, an intermittent water-
way on the edge of the Lachlan River catchment. A small
waterhole on Combaning Creek once supplied water to the
Comans family, Irish migrants who established a pastoral
property here in the 1840s, when Combaning lay on the edge
of the colonial frontier (see *fig. 1).* "Combaning" is derived
from the name given to this place by the local Wiradjuri people, and is recorded to mean "To hold water" (Tyrell 1933,
18). The name evokes an image of human hands cupped and
filled. To hold water is to honor its lively powers, to value it
deeply.

The Combaning district is one of the many productive
rural places in which we're all embedded, in real, ecological
ways. Before the arrival of British colonists, the fertile grassy
woodlands of the Combaning district nourished many generations of people. Since its development in the nineteenth and
twentieth centuries into modern, industrial farmland, wheat
and wool from paddocks in the Combaning region have fed

and kept warm millions of people in Australia and elsewhere. Ecological philosopher Val Plumwood evocatively described as "shadow places" those unseen terrains "that provide our material and ecological support" and "which, in a global market, are likely to elude our knowledge and responsibility" (Plumwood 2008, 139). The productive country that surrounds the Combaning waterhole can be considered one such "shadow place." Modern methods of agricultural production, processing and marketing ensure that few people whose bodies are nourished and warmed by Combaning produce are able to know this particular terrain that gives them life, or reciprocate the wellbeing it provides.

During the first decade of the twenty-first century, an intense drought, followed by widespread flooding, undermined the productive capacity of the Combaning region. Climate scientists predict ever more dramatic weather events across the inland of southeast Australia in the decades ahead. The Waterhole Project used storytelling and visual imagery to bring people into imaginative relationships with land and people, to allow the witnessing of suffering caused by the ecological disruptions of climate change. The project attempted to banish the shadows cast by industrial modernity across the Combaning district—a "shadow place" in the words of Plumwood—by emphasizing the material, ecological ties of people to one of the many productive rural places that nourish urban and country dwellers alike.

Modern understandings of human divorce from natural systems obscure pathways towards relationships of reciprocity between land and people. "Those who deny that nature and culture, landscape and politics, the city and the country are inextricably interfused have undermined that route for all of us," writes Rebecca Solnit (2007, 5). When the intimate, ecological ties of all people to the lands that warm and nourish them are denied, those lands lie vulnerable.

The Waterhole Project[1] sought to promote responsive re-

---

[1] The Waterhole Project (research weblog): http://nma.gov.au/blogs/waterhole/page/11/.

lationships by enabling a sense of connection to Combaning. Research and writing was presented online, in a blog format. Readers were invited to respond, to add their own ideas and stories. Links were presented to other institutions and bodies of knowledge. The style, method and structure of the research and its online presentation supported an argument about how we might respond to the crisis of climate change. The web structure of the blog format, the use of links and images, enabled a sense of connectivity and implied that in the face of climate change, ecological and social resilience depends on the forging of relationships.

Working as both an environmental historian and museum curator offers particular opportunities to critique problematic modern understandings of human separation from the rest of nature. In places and inside museums people encounter real, physical things. When we attend to places and to materiality, we undermine the "profound schism" imposed by Enlightenment science "between our intellectual convictions and the most basic conviction of our senses", writes David Abram, "between our mental concepts and our bodily percepts" (Abram 1997, 42). Physical encounters with places, objects and images allow our sensing bodies, as well as our minds, to make meanings. Places, objects and images communicate understandings that words alone cannot. They allow us to comprehend the experiences of others, to find an embodied knowledge of being (MacDougall 2006, 3–5).

In 1939, Elizabeth Sanderson bought a pair of high-heeled satin shoes from the exclusive London store Harrods (see *fig. 2).* They were part of an outfit the young Australian woman wore for her presentation to King George VI at Buckingham Palace. The outfit is now held by the National Museum of Australia in the National Historical Collection. Elizabeth Sanderson had grown up on Billabong station, a large sheep and cattle property beside Lake Cowal, a wide ephemeral lake downstream from the waterhole on Combaning Creek. Her family drew their wealth from land forcibly taken a century previously from the local Wiradjuri people. One clue to the violent processes that secured this particular locality for pastoral production is found in the memoirs of John McGuire, who as a young man supervised Billabong station in the 1840s. McGuire described how four pastoral runs at Lake Cowal, including Billabong, built their huts close to each other, in adjacent corners of the properties, so the station men could together defend themselves from attack by Wiradjuri (Pinkstone 2009).

Figure 2. Elizabeth Sanderson's shoes. Image courtesy of the National Museum of Australia.

When we situate Elizabeth Sanderson's shoes, and their provenance, within the context of place, of Billabong station and Lake Cowal, each informs our understandings of the other. We better understand the processes of Aboriginal dispossession and commodity production that enabled the purchase of these shoes, and we better understand the dynamics of colonial power and global trade that have reshaped the ecological and social realities of the Combaning area.

In her diary Elizabeth Sanderson described her presentation to King George amid the splendor of Buckingham Palace as "the most thrilling and wonderful event of my life" (National Museum of Australia, internal file). In London, at the very center of colonial power, Sanderson perceived much beauty and value. The collection associated with Elizabeth

Sanderson provides insights into cultural processes operating within Australian society that enabled ecological fragmentation in the Combaning region and elsewhere. The collection records the extent to which Australian settlers cast a distant place, Britain, the colonial center, as the primary source of cultural value and significance. These processes devalued local particularities and favored powerful demands and interests arising in faraway places. Today, market forces emanating from urban centers continue to give commercial demands priority above the ecological needs of rural places. Such forces still depend on the devaluing and erasure of local particularities.

Figure 3. Farming country beside Bland Creek, April 2010. Photograph by George Main.

I took the photograph above (see *fig.* 3) beside Bland Creek, upstream from Billabong station, towards Combaning. It shows the remains of two old eucalyptus trees that the landholder had recently bulldozed to make it easier for his massive farming equipment to sweep across the wide paddock. Here the forceful fragmentation of a local ecosystem continues, a process which, as Vandana Shiva argues, is integral to the binding of productive places to distant markets

(Shiva 1991, 248). Ecologists explain how the ongoing fragmentation of a local ecology makes land less resilient to extreme weather events and other shocks. As climate patterns become increasingly chaotic, we need more resilience, not less.

The hot and dry weather of recent years, and a series of crop failures, have spurred people in the Combaning region to find different ways of engaging with farmland. In their quest to remain productive, some farmers are turning towards native grasses—indigenous species highly adapted to drought and local conditions—that continue to grow inside hard worn paddocks. The Lake Cowal Foundation, a local conservation organization, invited farmers to participate in a series of pasture cropping trials. Pasture cropping involves the autumn sowing of cereal crops directly into native grass pasture. Through winter, crops emerge from beneath a protective cover of sturdy tussocks. Grazing by livestock is managed to promote the seeding and spread of native grasses in summer and autumn. Earthworms and other organisms vital to soil and plant health return beneath the grassy surface. Grain yields are usually lower, but so are input costs and risk, and production from grazing rises.

Pasture cropping involves turning towards and valuing local particularities—native grasses—in response to the local effects of a global phenomenon. It seems that farmers beside Lake Cowal are increasingly working within "an ancient set of alliances," as environmental historian Donald Worster describes the network of dynamic relationships that characterize a local ecology (Worster 1979, 66). Through the building of alliances, the work of Lake Cowal farmers suggest, we might find the resilience to survive the Anthropocene.

Museums hold powers to bring stories, materiality, places and people together, to build alliances. The Waterhole Project demonstrated the value of interactive virtual technologies to effect connections, to build resilience.

11: Food Connect(s)

Jenny Cameron and Robert Pekin

Much of our food does not taste good—and not just because apples have lost their crunch. The food we eat in the West is produced largely through an industrial model of agriculture. Larger and larger farms produce more and more of the one product, whether cattle or wheat, apricots or almonds, oranges or lemons. In the process, agricultural land is robbed of its nutrients, and animals and plants their dignity. But everywhere people, like Robert Pekin from Food Connect, are innovating with ways of working *with* the land, animals and others.

> At Food Connect, we're not just modifying, we're completely reinventing the business of how food should be done. We're saying that the old model is obsolete and we have to invent new ones. We have to restore ecological biodiversity back into our farming landscapes but we need a marketplace that recognizes and rewards the farmers who do this, and that encourages more farmers to do more of it.

People are developing all sorts of innovations around food production, distribution and consumption. Some initiatives *gift food*. For example, there are open community gardens where anyone can take the produce (even if they don't work in the gardens), and there are programs that use excess food from restaurants in meals for marginalized groups. Some initiatives *share food*. For example, in community kitchens anyone can come along and collectively cook and share food. Some initiatives *share land*. For example, in some urban neighborhoods, property owners share their land (even their front and backyards) with urban farmers and then share in the produce.

Then there are initiatives where the terms of trade reflect concerns about the well-being of those who work the land. For example, there are fair and direct trade arrangements that provide fair prices for small and marginalized farmers in the majority world. In the minority world, there are initiatives like Community Supported Agriculture that develop fair and direct trade arrangements with farmers, as Robert Pekin explains.

> Traditionally farmers send their produce to the market, and a buyer pays cash right there, as does the retailer and then the consumer. But the farmer doesn't get paid for sixty to ninety days. At Food Connect we've reversed all that.
>
> Our members pay a subscription in advance. Some of them pay twelve months in advance. And we pay the farmer on the knocker when they deliver the produce. And the farmer sets the price.
>
> This is how it works. Because our members pay in advance, we have a big spreadsheet of what we need at different times of the year and we say to a farmer "There's a window of opportunity to grow something for us here in November, it would be great if it was something green. You work out what the price is that you want, set it flat and come back and tell us." And the farmer will go "Beauty! Normally at the peak of the season I get this price, but then we have to pay all these costs and really I'm only selling 60 percent of my crop because the market will only accept a certain look. With

Food Connect I'm now going to sell 100 percent of my crop because they'll take a bit of leaf damage or hail damage. And I don't have to grade my produce. And I can reuse my boxes. And they're going to consolidate my freight because I can send it in with other farmers. And then there's all the other intangibles. They're going to connect me with other farmers because at Food Connect they encourage farmers to work together and learn from each other, and not see each other as competitors."

We're taking farmers out of the business-as-usual economic paradigm that provides no security around the price. The farmer sets a flat price that we pay when the produce is delivered. And it also means that farmers instead of investing in say $250,000 to $500,000 for a grading machine can invest in looking after the land.

The diverse economic practices that we're seeing reflect a growing awareness of the interdependencies between producers and consumers. In the case of Community Supported Agriculture initiatives like Food Connect, the interdependency is so strong that consumers pay in advance and thereby agree to share the risks of agriculture with the farmer—hence, some people now refer to it as Community *Shared* Agriculture. We're also seeing how the closer relationship between producer and consumer can support and encourage farming practices that are more environmentally sustainable.

For farmers in Food Connect the real incentive is the contact with the people who eat their food. We run farm tours to our growers. And every time our farmers cannot stop talking. They have never had so many questions about what they do or been so acknowledged. Farmers are almost in tears because people have come out to see what they do and they have hugged them and thanked them. People say, "I love what you're doing to your land. I love that you've got this nature strip over there, and you preserve this wetland area, and that you've got this field lying fallow over there, and you're growing this great produce, and you're doing it all without chemicals."

We just had a farm tour two weeks ago and I was talking to the honey grower afterwards and he said "I got all these thank-you cards." How many farmers get thank you cards from the people who eat their produce?

Figure 1. "Franco believes great kohlrabi comes from listening to its needs." Photograph by Adam Sebastian West.[1]

Another set of critical relationships are those in the "work" places that are scattered along the chain of connection between producer and consumer. These workplaces range from the volunteer groups who manage and run community gardens and community kitchens to the centers of formal paid employment. Just as an ethic of care can characterize relationships between producers, consumers and the environment, so too we can find an ethic of care in these workplaces.

Money is not a great measure of happiness or feeling that your life is contributing to something whilst you're on Planet Earth. So within Food Connect we talk in

[1] Source: Food Connect, http://www.foodconnect.com.au/.

terms of a living wage. We ask what is a living wage? And we're exploring that question openly with everyone at Food Connect. So we work backwards from saying that a living wage means being able to send your kids to the school they want, and to buy or have a house.

We have also decided that people need to be paid differently because there are "responsibles": people who make weighty decisions around the business and finances; there are the coordinators who harmonize things and coordinate the doing; and then there are the co-workers, people who do the leg work. So we have a hierarchy, but it's a horizontal hierarchy with some people out front breaking new ground and others coming along behind pulling it all together. We've decided to have no more than a two to one ratio between the highest and lowest pay rates.

We're doing a couple of other things. We are a not-for-profit company limited by shares, and the only shareholders are our workers. Once someone has been at Food Connect for three years they can become a shareholder.

We also have seasonal reviews at Food Connect. So the co-workers evaluate the coordinators, the coordinators evaluate the responsibles, and the responsibles evaluate the board of management. But in the evaluation process people are saying, "Oh, this is what it takes to become a coordinator or a responsible." So by osmosis they're actually starting to learn the skills and qualities they need to develop if they want to be a coordinator or a responsible.

Some of the apples might have lost their crunch, but there is work going on across the planet to produce food in ways that will sustain the environment and nurture humans. Living— and eating—in the Anthropocene means connecting with and committing to these innovative practices that are foregrounding the interdependencies between humans and between humans and the planet.

With these interdependencies you have to think less about yourself and more about others. And this is a struggle, but that's what's needed at the moment. If you're serious about changing what humans have done to the environment and to other people, you have to step up to the mark and enter into a higher order of relationships with others and with the planet.

EXAMPLES OF INITIATIVES

Community Gardening:

Newcastle Community Garden Project,
http://ps3beta.com/project/7733

Community Kitchens:

Kumera Community Kitchen
http://kumerakitchen.blogspot.com/

Land Sharing:

Landshare
http://www.landshare.net/

Fair and Direct Trade:

Alter Trade Japan
http://www.altertrade.co.jp/english/index-e.html

Community Supported Agriculture:

Food Connect
http://www.foodconnect.com.au/

Beanstalk
http://beanstalk.org.au/

12: GRAFFITI IS LIFE

KURT IVESON

The challenge of living in the Anthropocene is, for the majority of the world's population, an urban challenge. Finding ways to connect with each other and our urban environments is an essential task. Where might we find examples of an "ethics of care" taking shape in our cities to inspire us in meeting this challenge? An inner-city meatworks carpark covered in graffiti might be the last place we would think to look. But the story of how such a carpark became, for a time, the Graffiti Hall of Fame has plenty to teach us as we seek out new ways of inhabiting and caring for our urban environments.

In the narratives of urban decline and renewal that permeate contemporary urban policy discussions, graffiti writers frequently feature as villains. Graffiti is seen as a form of dirt, decay, and destruction, perpetrated by anti-social vandals who lack respect for the sanctity of property and community.

And yet, as anyone who has spent any time with graffiti writers will know, this is not how many of them see themselves or their craft. In fact, graffiti writers and artists care a great deal about the city, its accessibility, its aesthetics and its atmosphere. To them, graffiti makes the city better. Seen through a graffiti writer's eyes, trains, abandoned buildings, and blank walls simply look better with graffiti. The individual, if illicit, inscriptions on neighborhood walls are seen as signs of life, not of decay. Indeed, graffiti tends to flourish in spaces planners often describe as "dead zones"—while the planners are waiting for injections of capital to bring such places back to "life", graffiti writers give them another kind life by injecting them with color, style and energy.

Perhaps most importantly, many graffiti writers consider themselves to be participating in a cultural movement, and this movement has a profound connection with, and respect for, the city. To participate in this culture is to become an urban explorer. The practice of writing graffiti necessitates a very close engagement with circulatory systems and surfaces of the city, with its opportunities and constraints, and with its others. To participate in this culture is also to embrace (and sometimes debate) rules about which surfaces are up for grabs, and which are off-limits. While these rules might not conform to the law as it stands, this does not signal an absence of ethics. This is why private cars and memorials are rarely written on, and why other graffiti writers will be among the harshest critics when they are.

Urban authorities typically fail to recognize these cultural and ethical dimensions of graffiti, and its consequent criminalization becomes a catch-22. Policies which further criminalize graffiti writing have not stopped it, but they have pushed writers and their culture further underground, thereby hampering the development and dissemination of these ethical principles within the graffiti writing scene, as well as precluding casual encounters between graffiti writers and other publics in the city.

And yet, this misrecognition of graffiti is by no means universal. One example of how the city might channel, rather than obstruct, the energies and ethics of graffiti writers is the old Graffiti Hall of Fame in Sydney (see *fig. 1*). About twenty years ago Tony Spanos, the owner of a meatworks on Botany Road, Alexandria, made his car park and its walls available for local kids. Graffiti used to pop up every now and again, and having had a colorful childhood himself, Spanos knew better than to fear the kids who were expressing themselves on his walls. Concerned about the growing criminalization of these graffiti writers, Spanos wanted to give them some breathing space in the inner city where they could paint and create with permission.

Figure 1. The Graffiti Hall of Fame in its heyday. Photograph by Matthew Peet (used with permission).

The space blossomed. As word spread, some of the best graffiti artists in the city started to frequent Spanos' car park, which came to be known as the Graffiti Hall of Fame. It also played host to dance parties and other kinds of gatherings. A vacant space beside a meatworks in an industrial area had come to life, as new connections between people and place were made. The Graffiti Hall of Fame sustained a particular way of living in, and caring for, the city. As Spanos put it once in an interview in the *Sydney Morning Herald* (19 November 1999, 9): "a car park is all I have given these kids and they created their own energy. The Government has billions of dollars and all they needed was a car park in a meatworks."

Eventually, the trouble came to be that there was a little too much life in this carpark. Inevitably, as this part of Botany Road was re-zoned from industrial to commercial and residential, the space became the subject of complaints and legal challenges by new residents. It was finally shut down by a decision of the Land and Environment Court. A block of apartments has recently been constructed where it once stood.

The loss of the Graffiti Hall of Fame still reverberates for those who remember it. It's not just that things changed, but the manner of the change, that rankles. As ever, the planners and courts simply could not see anything happening here. The carpark was simply vacant land, awaiting redevelopment, with no proper use. Just as surely as irrigation of the Murray River helped to destroy Indigenous connections to country, in this instance gentrification and misrecognition helped to break down a youthful culture of care for the inner-urban environment.

And yet, this culture persists, even in the face of its ongoing criminalization. And there continue to be those like Spanos who can see the writing on the wall for what it is. A couple of suburbs away from Alexandria, in St Peters, Tugi Balog has recently made the large wall of his business available to graffiti writers and street artists, and he has invited his neighbors to do the same (see *fig. 2*). When the explosion of colorful, and often chaotic, work in May Lane attracted the inevitable complaints, Marrickville Council conducted a survey of local residents. Over 80 percent thought that the art added character to their area, and they wanted this "outdoor gallery" to survive.

Figure 2. Graffiti on May Lane, Sydenham, Sydney. Photograph by Kurt Iveson.

Of course, not everyone likes graffiti, and that's just fine. The point, rather, is that those authorities and property owners who are busy painting urban surfaces various shades of brown and beige don't have a monopoly on caring for the city. Graffiti writers care too—deeply, in many cases. Life in cities inevitably produces such scenes of disagreement. And figuring out how to deal with these disagreements politically, rather than through police action and communitarian closure, surely constitutes one of our most important projects for the Anthropocene. This politics can only take place if we are attuned to the many forms of life which shape and depend upon our urban environments. Capital is by no means the only source of energy and life that will sustain them.

13: Flying Foxes in Sydney

Do city dwellers dream of wide open spaces like rangelands, or do they dream of tall buildings? Do their dreams entice them to look up into the great, blue depths above them, and do flying foxes flit across the night sky of their sleep? Do they ever think: "now, this is a biodiver-city!"?

At least one city dweller, journalist James Woodford, looked up with delight. He wrote: "watching bats silhouetted against the stars is one of the greatest, but little known, pleasures of life" (Woodford 2003). Actually, many city dwellers find pleasure in the fact that their city and their lives are shared with flying foxes. Every night around sunset the flying foxes start their nightly flyout. With their dark fur, their wingspans of up to one meter, and their distinctive bat silhouette, they stand out against the clear colors of an Australian sunset. They are beautiful wherever they are, but in Sydney, Australia's largest and most iconic city, they are fantastic! They span out across the Opera House, and over the Harbour Bridge. One can sit at Circular Quay, sipping a drink and watching the ferries, the bridge, and the lights of Luna Park flashing across the harbor. Then the motion above begins. The gaze that has been fixed horizontally shifts upward to the blizzard of flying foxes, and one feels quite close to paradise.

Figure 1. A grey headed flying fox. Photograph courtesy of Nick Edards.

The flying foxes who live in Sydney are mostly *Pteropus poliocephalus*—grey headed flying foxes. They and their kin are chiropterans, meaning "hand winged." There are two Sub-orders: mega and micro. Worldwide, megachiroptera include 166 species of flying foxes (also known as fruit bats) and blossom bats. Microchiroptera include 759 species. The two Sub-orders are quite different, size being only part of it. Microchiroptera navigate by echolocation (animal sonar); they are small and feed mainly on insects but there also are blood-eating vampire bats, fish-eating bats, and other carnivorous bats. In contrast, megachiroptera all feed on plants. They navigate principally by sight, and many of them are large. In Australia, the largest male flying foxes weigh about one kilogram (2.2 pounds) and have wingspans of up to 1.5 meters (nearly five feet) (Hall and Richards 2000, 1–3).

There is no way of knowing the flying fox population figures prior to British settlement of Australia, but certainly the numbers would have been in the thousands of millions. Four main species of flying foxes make up the Australian contingent: Black Flying Fox (*Pteropus Alecto*), Grey-headed Flying Fox (*P. poliocephalus*), Little Red Flying Fox (*P. scapulatus*), and Spectacled Flying Fox (*P. conspicillatus*). By preference they travel widely in search of pollen, seeds and fruits, covering vast areas every year as they follow flowering and fruiting trees and shrubs. At this time, both grey-headed and spectacled flying foxes are listed as threatened under the Commonwealth Environment Protection and Biodiversity Conservation Act 1999.

The situation for grey headed flying foxes is grave. Their numbers are plummeting, and in spite of the fact that they are a protected species, they are legally shot by orchardists who are issued licenses to do so. The licenses are issued by the same organization that has the legislative responsibility to protect them. In Sydney they are not shot, but that does not mean that everyone welcomes them. The CBD (Central Business District) flying foxes camp by day in the Royal Botanic Gardens adjacent to the circular quay area where they are a huge tourist attraction. All day people stream through the Gardens looking for the flying foxes, photographing them, and watching in awe as they scrabble around in their trees, squabble, have sex, raise babies, and generally live their daytime lives in full view of a completely captivated, ever-changing audience. In the late afternoons, as families stroll along the lagoon or have tea on the open lawn, flying foxes swoop down to the lagoon, belly dipping across the surface and then flying back to their branch where they settle and lick the water off their tummy fur. One could hardly imagine a more congenial example of multi-species conviviality in the city.

Part of what makes the situation so dire for flying foxes is that the Royal Botanic Gardens (RBG) authorities do not want them to be there. Flying foxes have made their camps in a number of exotic trees with heritage value, and their camp is wrecking the trees. So severe is the commitment of the

RBG to ridding the Gardens of flying foxes that they have applied for, and been granted, permission from the Federal Minister for the Environment to expel the flying foxes. They have thirty years in which to accomplish total removal. Because these creatures are endangered, and because this is a maternity camp, there are restrictions on the actions that can be taken. The bottom line is clear, though: the RBG can do its best to stress them to the point where they simply give up. No one knows or can predict where they may go, who may next feel annoyed and decide to get rid of them, and whether this effort will turn into a dynamic of cascading death.

The determination on the part of the RBG to get rid of the flying foxes is counterbalanced by the flying foxes commitment to their camp. These creatures are notorious for their site fidelity. A good camp must, of course, be situated so that food is within nightly commuting distance. This means that food will generally be within a range of up to fifty kilometers round trip per night (Eby 1991, 547). Other considerations include water, microclimate (especially in summer), and probably ease of navigation (Hall and Richards 2000, 61). We have no way of knowing how many good camps have been destroyed in the two hundred years of British settlement, but we know it must be proportional to the loss of native habitat, i.e., between 70 percent and 95 percent (Eby 1995, 31). We also have no insight into the impacts on flying foxes when they return to a home camp only to find that it has been destroyed. Nor do we know how flying foxes go about deciding on a new camp. The best we can say is that they do it. Once they make a decision, they stick to it with awesome determination.

One flying fox expert and carer, Tim Pearson, describes the RBG situation as a watershed moment in the life of the species. He believes that if the RBG is successful in expelling the flying foxes, other local and regional councils will be encouraged to see expulsion as a legitimate way of avoiding having to learn to live with and amongst flying foxes. Within a matter of decades, there may be no grey headed flying foxes with whom anyone will have the opportunity to share their city and their lives.

This current moment of cleansing, in which humans decide to rid their neighborhood of those they don't like, is startlingly familiar. Flying foxes are involved in most of the major catastrophic events of contemporary life on Earth: warfare, man-made mass death, famine, urbanization, emerging diseases, climate change, and biosecurity. At the same time, they are targeted for aid and rescue through conservation programs and local/international non-government organization aid. They are endangered, and are involved in all four of the major factors causing extinctions: habitat loss, overexploitation, introduced species, and extinction cascades.

An account of flying foxes in Sydney exposes many complexities of relationships amongst living things in this time of mounting stress. As Donna Haraway stated with great elegance: "we and others are entangled in knots of species and are co-shaping each other in layers of reciprocating complexity" (Haraway 2008, 42). A particularly vivid example of entangled knots of species concerns threats to flying foxes in and around orchards. Two scientists, Martin and McIlwee, work with the metaphor of a black hole in analyzing the dynamics of population loss (Martin and McIlwee 2002, 105). They offer the term "pteropucide" as a descriptor of the man-made mass death inflicted upon flying foxes. Their scathing analysis of attempts to eradicate flying foxes from a given area offers an understanding of why orchardists can claim that the numbers of flying foxes are increasing while scientists claim that the numbers are decreasing. Orchards (or any other places that offer food) function as a vortex that draws more and more flying foxes into it. The "pteropucidal black hole" dynamic depends on the fact that every place which affords food and in which local populations have been eradicated entices more animals. "The culling produces a local vacant niche, which becomes occupied by animals moving into it from further afield, which are then killed, so producing a local vacant niche which . . . and so on" (Martin and McIlwee 2002, 105). They refer to such kill/attract/kill zones as pteropucidal, and they attest that the dynamic is like "an irresistible gravitational force sweeping everything into its maw." The inexorable dynamic works with the forces of starvation that drive flying foxes into orchards; zones of attraction become zones of injury, suffering and death (Martin and McIlwee 2002). At the same time, flying foxes are targeted for dispersal not only in orchards, but in many places, including the Royal Botanic Gardens. Camps are dispersed, groups are harassed and stressed, flying foxes become trapped in areas where they starve or feed on food that brings them into peril—it goes on and on.

The metaphor of gravitational draw is powerful in itself, and can be taken further: the pteropucidal black hole does not have a boundary that stops with flying foxes. Flying foxes are key pollinators and seed dispersers, and when they are dragged into the vortex of death, forests and other ecosystems are dragged along with them. This means that critically endangered ecosystems may be dragged into the vortex, and so will the rare and endangered animals who live in them—cassowaries, for example, along with a number of mammals, frogs, and other creatures. As is well known, rainforests are colloquially referred to as the "lungs" of the planet, soaking up carbon dioxide and pumping out oxygen (Fyfe 2005). As rainforests disappear, so does the possibility of sustaining an Earth system that will be inhabitable for large numbers of the species of beings who have evolved here and belong here.

Of course the black hole does not exempt humans, and this is so in direct ways as well as in the prospect of losing Earth's habitable climate and atmosphere. Three significant new zoonotic viruses (transmissible between humans and animals) have emerged in flying fox populations: Hendra virus, Menangle virus and Lyssavirus. Of these, Lyssavirus is potentially the most serious in its impacts on humans; it is closely related to rabies, and has demonstrably been transmitted from a flying fox to a human. It is unclear to what extent Lyssavirus may transfer to other mammal populations. These new viruses may have been present in flying fox populations for a long time, but have changed into active agency in recent years probably as a result of stress (Hume Field, quoted in Booth et al. 2008, 17), and the Lyssavirus is most likely to be found in animals already sick or stressed (Hall and Richards 2000, 56–57). With these emerging diseases harm may come full circle, demonstrating the inextricable connectivities between human health, flying fox health, and habitat health (Macdonald and Laurenson 2006).

The vortex keeps growing. More stress means more sick flying foxes, more sickness means more flying foxes in need of rescue and more people seeking to help distressed flying foxes. The language of public hygiene and biosecurity gains new force, and vilification of flying foxes gains new ammunition. The best answer, as Booth and others point out, is to "conserve flying foxes and reduce the environmental stresses—including shooting—that increase their rate of infection and the risk of spillover to other species" (Booth 2008, 17). If, however, the human response is to accelerate the stresses in an effort to control the boundary between humans and flying foxes, the feedback loop takes on the shape and dynamics of the vortex. Cascades of death mark out a deathscape of disastrous, entangled, recursive devastation.

Positioned, like much of life on Earth today, in enlarging zones of conflict and terror, the lives and deaths of flying foxes tell us that in the Anthropocene there is no way out of entanglements within multi-species communities. Rather than seeking to erect more impenetrable barriers against others, relational ethics for living and dying in the Anthropocene urge us to assume ever greater mutuality and accountability as intra-dependent members of the suffering family of life on Earth.

POSTSCRIPT

After this essay was written, the Royal Botanic Gardens started its program to force the flying foxes from their home places. The work, if such a benign term can be used in this context, continues.

14: EARTH AS ETHIC

FREYA MATHEWS

In this era of climate change when upheavals of a global nature are set to sweep the planet, the need for global agreements that transcend the strict proportionalities of national
interest is greater than ever before. Different nations of
course have different degrees of vulnerability to environmental disruption and different degrees of economic wherewithal
to mitigate or manage it. Those with the greatest economic
means happen also, with some exceptions (such as Australia),
to be those least vulnerable, at least in the short to medium
term. As long as self-interest rules the day then, nations with
the most to contribute to climate mitigation will tend to hold
back and international agreements will be pre-empted or
fatally weakened, with dire consequences in the longer term
for all.

This scenario can be avoided only if the commitment un-
dertaken by all nations to mitigate and ultimately reverse
climate change is a moral and not merely a self-interested
one. Nations need to acknowledge that de-stabilizing the
planetary climate system is monumentally morally wrong
and that we have a moral responsibility to mitigate and repair
the damage. But how can such moral agreement be obtained
in a multicultural world of rampantly competing ideologies

in which different moral "truths" define different moral constituencies? Is it possible to imagine an international society morally united in its commitment to the integrity of the biosphere?

Such moral accord will never be produced merely by reason, as different cultures reason from different premises. Moral truth is hatched inside stories, specifically stories about the nature of the universe, the whys and wherefores of creation. Such stories, which are always normative in their implications, provide the founding narratives for religions: different stories lead to different religions, different religions to different moral truths. Is it possible to imagine a common story? Science is already of course to some degree a common story. But it tells us that the universe unfolds in accordance with causal laws rather than moral meanings. The normative implication of this is that we can ultimately do as we please: we are not bound by responsibilities to the cosmos. Self-interest rules. So science does not appear in any ultimate sense to advance the moral cause.

As it happens however, in this very hour of our greatest moral need, a new story is coming into view, a story made visible by the environmental crisis itself. This is the story of the earth, of the biosphere. It is a story of stories, a larger story made up of a vast intersection of little stories, each little story being the story of an individual life. Notice that story, as a form, recapitulates the basic structure of a life: beginning, middle, end. The organism is born, strives against radical uncertainty to perpetuate its life, to postpone its death, but death is inevitable and sooner or later, whatever the organism does, death brings the story to an end. The middle of the story is fraught with intense suspense as the organism struggles to carve out a limited space for its existence. It is this striving, this purpose, this normativity, which draws otherwise random events into the patterns of coherence—of meaning—that mark out the terrain of narrative. In its striving for existence, the individual provides the mattering that brings meaning into the world. The life of the individual is thus the prototype of story itself. This is presumably why we find the narrative form so compelling: we are caught up by the suspense of a story—where suspense is one of the key ingredients of storytelling—because that suspense reproduces, in microcosm and in a cathartic way, the suspense and radical moment-to-moment uncertainty of our own existence. This is presumably also why, when the story is finished, we very quickly lose interest in the plot and characters; as soon as the ending is known the story ceases to hook into the suspense of our own existence. But while story recapitulates the structure of the life of the individual, there is a larger story of which the individual is in fact only part. The larger story, we can now see, is likewise one of striving against uncertainty to stave off extinction and perpetuate the conditions for self-existence, but this is a striving enacted at the level of the greater whole, the biosphere. And the vital point about this greater story is that it not only draws otherwise random events into patterns of coherence, thereby creating meaning, as individual stories do; the patterns of coherence it creates are inherently *moral*. Final extinction is perpetually postponed by way of an exquisite attunement of all beings to the needs of others. All beings desire what other beings need them to desire. Honeybees desire nectar, and in the process of getting it pollinate the flowers which supply it. Bettongs desire truffles, and in the process of digging for them aerate the forest soils that sustain them. Emus desire zamia nuts, and in the process of digesting them prepare them for germination. Everyone in this proto-story serves themselves by serving others. The proto-story is simultaneously a proto-ethics. Meaning at its root it is not only narrative and normative but proto-moral: do-unto-others is hatched within the story of the earth.

Such a pre-established harmony of mutually enfolded desires is only *proto*-ethical because in the biosphere it has resulted from natural selection rather than conscious choice. Nevertheless, it provides a clear template for an ethics of conscious choice. As such a template it is the forgotten touchstone of all religion. All religion is animated by the impulse to create meaning via story and by an intuition of the essentially normative and ethical character of story: stories tell us how to live, and the "moral" of story is indeed moral: we live by enabling others to live. The spiritual truth at the heart of religion is thus an earth-truth. We live, whether as individuals or as species, by desiring what others need us to desire. This is a truth consistent with science, since it is about the organization of the biosphere. But it is not reducible to science, because it creates the conditions for meaning within which alone science can itself come into existence.

Figure 1. Our earth root as the basis of all morality and meaning.
Photograph by John Clar.

This earth-truth, at once scientific and spiritual, is one that belongs to us all, regardless of cultural provenance. It is becoming visible now because it has been so sorely breached. We have not observed the proto-ethic. We have not desired what the biosphere needs us to desire. So the conditions for life are not being perpetuated. The honeybees are leaving, forsaking not only our crops but the wild plants that depend on them for fertilization. The shells of foraminifera, microscopic marine animals, are thinning as a result of the acidification of the oceans, placing in doubt the future of the entire marine food pyramid, of which foraminifera form the base. Starving creatures, such as polar bears, are resorting to eating their young, ensuring their own extinction. Legions of other species are in retreat as the sixth great extinction event in the history of our planet gets into full swing. There are vast fire-storms and other wild atmospheric phantasms on our horizon. Self-interest is manifestly a withered stalk supporting us. It is time we remembered that only our earth root, the root of all morality and meaning, will sustain us, and that it is our common heritage. Let us bring this, and not our cultural differences, to the negotiating table. Let us allow a new civilization to emerge, a civilization of many colors, many cultures, many religions, yes, but also of an underlying moral accord sprung from our shared origin in the newly visible story behind all stories, the proto-story of how beings, in all the intricacy of their particularity, nevertheless live only by enabling other beings to live.

Researching with Others

15: ON EXPERIMENTATION

JENNY CAMERON

In 1957, the American scientists Roger Revelle and Hans Suess wrote that, "human beings are now carrying out a large-scale geophysical experiment of a kind that could not have happened in the past nor be reproduced in the future" (quoted in Hulme and Mahony 2010, 706). They were of course talking about our experiment with global industrial development and the release of millions of tons of greenhouse gases into the atmosphere. As we now know, it is an experiment that is starting to produce disastrous consequences on a global scale. We have truly been playing with fire and it is increasingly evident that we are being burned. As a result many of us are going to have to make major shifts in how we live our lives or, sooner or later, those shifts will be forced on us as the world changes and adapts around us. The future is scarily unknown.

What role can social research play in coming to terms with a future in which the certainties of the past have gone and the future lies before us unknown?

If we are now living in a planetary experiment, perhaps social research could also take a more experimental approach. By this I do not mean the sort of carefully controlled experiment where we isolate and test variables to try and determine cause and effect. Rather I'm thinking of more open, even playful forms, of experimentation to try out new ways of living in the Anthropocene.

Such an approach would mean setting aside the idea of research as a neutral and objective activity in which there is critical distance between the researcher and the object of study. Instead, research would entail making a stand for certain worlds and for certain ways of living on the planet, and taking responsibility for helping to make these worlds more likely and these ways of living more widespread.

Despite the scariness of these times, this type of experimental research requires a hopeful stance initially as we look for glimmers of possible worlds and ways of living with human and non-human others, and then as we devise ways for our research to help make these glimmers stronger. An ethics of researching in the Anthropocene therefore means not just foregrounding the realities our research is helping to build, but also attending to how our research methods might help to bring these realities into being.

These research "methods" might involve working alongside others who in their everyday lives are trying out and experimenting with new practices for new worlds. This would mean forming the types of hybrid research collectives made up of the academic and "lay" researchers that Roelvink discusses in this volume. Perhaps we might work with lay researchers to help articulate and delineate what they are doing by drawing on our skills of connecting and framing. Perhaps we might work with lay researchers to help sharpen and strengthen what they are doing by applying our critical aptitude in a generous and creative spirit. Perhaps we might work with lay researchers to help broadcast what they are doing by turning our skills in communicating and teaching to new contexts.

None of this means that we have to respond to the planetary experiment at an equally planetary scale. The scale of these experiments by lay researchers may be small; and the scale of our academic research may be also small. And well may they stay that way, for the risk of things that are "joined-up," "rolled-out" or "scaled-up" is that we replicate on a global scale the one approach or model—as we have done with the current economic and technological development pathway that has gotten us into this situation. Instead, let us respond to the planetary experiment that so many across the globe (human and non-human) are unwittingly caught up in by proliferating small-scale experiments that might offer multiple openings and avenues for new ways of living.

Figure 1. Academic and lay researchers learning about each other's community garden experiments. Photograph by Jenny Cameron.

Let us also take to heart the idea that our research is an *open* experiment. Our experimental social research approach is not aimed at establishing and entrenching an end point and knowledge certainty. For a long time, the world will be changing and adapting around us, and we are going to have to respond and adjust. This understanding helps to take us away from the notion that our research has to be oriented towards determining whether things are a success or failure. Instead we will be experimenting in and with an ever-changing and uncertain world that is going to throw up surprises some of which will seem to stymie possibilities but some of which will offer new possibilities. As experimental social researchers these are the possibilities we need to be attuned to and responsive to.

16: Reading for Difference

J.K. Gibson-Graham

It seems that rats have something to teach us humans at this point in the history of our species, at least that's what I am hearing. In *The End of the Long Summer* Dianne Dumanoski tells us that "for most of the human career ... we have shared far more with rats: another species of nimble, flexible generalists and remarkable survivors" (Dumanoski 2009, 173). It's only in the modern era of carboniferous capitalism, since most societies have hitched their fortunes to a fossil-fuel based growth strategy, that our species has become less rat-like—less nimble, less flexible, more specialist and increasingly less likely to survive the changes we have wrought on our Earth system. The irony is stark—as the behavioral distance between rats and humans grows, so the "more evolved" species becomes increasingly vulnerable to the kinds of environmental shocks that rats have successfully weathered. *We* teeter on the edge of extinction, *they* are ready to ride out the "end of the long summer."

Indeed, the survivability of rats and the proliferation of different types of rodents over the evolutionary *longue durée* offers a corrective to popular conceptions of evolutionary development. As Stephen Jay Gould points out:

Who ever heard of the evolutionary trend of rodents or of

bats or of antelopes? Yet these are the greatest success stories in the history of mammals. Our proudest cases do not become our classic illustrations because we can draw no ladder of progress through a vigorous bush with hundreds of surviving twigs. (Gould 1991, 180)

In *The End of Capitalism (As We Knew It)* J.K. Gibson-Graham was inspired by Gould to pose this analogous question:

Who ever heard of the development in the contemporary western world of non-capitalist class processes like feudalism or slavery as prevalent forms of exploitation, or of independent commodity production as a locus of "self-appropriation"? Yet these are the greatest survival stories in the history of class. (Gibson-Graham 1996, 116)

We could learn a lot from the survivability and evolutionary flexibility of non-capitalist economic activities. But the flashy achievements of capitalist enterprise and exploitation over the last 200 years or so and the dismal science of economics have seduced us into believing that capitalist business sits on the top rung of a ladder of development which all economies seeking improvement must climb.

Currently it is the shrill voices of corporate capitalist CEOs who most oppose policy measures to reduce our carbon footprint and attempt to halt the imbalances that fossil fuel-reliant industry and agriculture are producing in our biosphere. These corporate citizens represent their companies as leaders in economic efficiency and value creation— top of the ladder in terms of adaptation to risk and opportunity. The disregard for the ecological context of their activities is likened to a form of "cultural autism" by Dumanoski (quoting Thomas Berry). As she puts it:

much of the behavior considered normal by the current global civilization appears pathological in light of our growing emergency—the unquestioned pursuit of exponential economic growth, the celebration of greed, wildly excessive consumption, radical individualism, overweening belief in human power, refusal to acknowledge limits, blind faith in salvation by technology, and the primacy among values of profit and efficiency. (Dumanoski 2009, 217)

Prompted by Gould we might reflect on why we imagine capitalist enterprise to be at the frontier of economic evolution, when it is the very form of enterprise whose lineage has brought us to the brink of extinction.

The accepted story of economic evolution is one of the emergence of ever more efficient, more competitive and therefore dominant forms of capitalist enterprise. But in the interstices of capitalist economic organization there lurk vibrant and timeless forms of self-employment and small business, family feudalism and slave enterprise, and non-market relations like gift-giving, reciprocity and unpaid caring labor. Added to this are more recent experiments with worker-owned cooperatives, state enterprise and social enterprise, fair-trade and community land trusts. Indeed, over time an increasingly diverse economic landscape has evolved in which capitalist enterprise, "free" markets, waged and salaried labor, private property and mainstream finance coexist with a plethora of non-capitalist economic activities. The lock step ladder of "progressive" economic development that sees competitive capitalism replacing feudalism, monopoly capitalism replacing competitive capitalism, and post-Fordism replacing Fordist capitalism runs a metaphorical steamroller over the copiously branching bushes of non-capitalist activity. Is it possible that these flexibly branching rodent-like practices might hold the key to rethinking economic survivability?

Significant contributions to wellbeing are made by non-capitalist or alternative capitalist enterprises, alternatively paid and unpaid labor, collectively owned and open access property, alternative markets and non-market transactions, and alternative and non-market finance. When we open up our blinkered research gaze we see a "diverse" economy comprised of activities that produce and distribute material well-being in all economies both those situated at the "bottom" of the development ladder as well as those at the "top." Many of these diverse activities involve trust, cooperation and mutual respect between humans and between humans and their living environment, and it is these that have "helped our ancestors survive past calamities" (Dumanoski 2009, 8).

Training ourselves to read for economic difference, not dominance, involves a very different research practice. Such a practice is not easy to maintain when one story of "capitalist" economic identity reigns. To read for difference, we must abandon a *capitalocentric* conceptual frame in which all economic activity is measured up against capitalist forms and seen as basically the same as, the opposite of, a complement to, or contained within capitalism (Gibson-Graham 1996, 6). We must construct a different vocabulary and language of economy that can register the variety of ways in which economic goods are produced, transacted, distributed, financed and owned.

When we take an appreciative, descriptive, and less systemic approach to our economic world we are able to see specific geographies and histories of economic interaction. We can begin to discern ethical practices of economy that maintain, sustain and enlarge ways of living well together with each other and earth others. Once we reveal a diverse economic landscape we can begin to track and theorize the economic dynamics we might like to encourage.

As in all ecosystems, economic diversity can create resilience. Diversity means that there are many different kinds of economic activity, some of which perform the same job. This doubling up is called functional redundancy and it provides insurance against disaster. Take the example of child care, which is performed in capitalist child care centers, community cooperative centers, volunteer neighborhood groups, extended, nuclear and single parent families (Cameron and Gibson-Graham 2003). In some contexts it is paid for, in others there is an audited system of reciprocity, and in yet others it is gifted and sometimes coerced. When a monopoly capitalist steel plant is closed down, steel is no longer produced in a region. But when a capitalist child care center goes bankrupt and closes, as did hundreds of centers owned by the company ABC Learning in Australia in 2008, the diverse economy of child care, though stretched, is ready to absorb the burden and continue to service this need. In this particular case a newly formed consortium of non-profit organizations stepped in to take over 678 of the more than 700 closed private capitalist centers, reopening them as social enterprises (Mission Australia 2009). The diversity of enterprise forms in the childcare "industry" was increased and sectoral resilience strengthened.

Figure 1. Succulent and cactus diversity, Norrköping, Sweden. Photograph by Katherine Gibson.

In general, the greater the variety in any sector of enterprise forms, ways of performing and remunerating labor, accessing property, transacting (sharing, giving and exchanging) and financing (saving and borrowing), the less vulnerable an economy is to crisis and stress. That's not to say that economic diversity is an unquestioned good. This is pretty obvious in a world where child slavery, indentured labor, theft, feudal tenancy, financial extortion or super-exploitative capitalist enterprises are part of the diverse economy. A resilient economy is one where there is life-giving synergy be-tween diverse economic activities—where nurturing and convivial habitats, both social and natural, are reproduced and maintained. It is one where ethical considerations must guide economic calculation.

As researchers we are challenged to ask: what kinds of economic dynamics might support such developments and co-developments? In her last book *The Nature of Economies*, Jane Jacobs brought bio-mimicry to bear on the question of economic development. Just as permaculture consciously designs "agriculturally productive ecosystems which have the diversity, stability and resilience of natural ecosystems" (Mollison 1988, ix), so Jacobs asks us to imagine regional economies designed around the self-refueling growth of a diverse range of economic activities (Jacobs 2000, 68). As each develops it has the potential to enhance the interde-pendent growth of other activities that build up a region into a relatively self-sufficient unit. While sectors of economic activity might be connected to global, non-local economic activities by ethically directed terms of trade, migration and financial flow, they would be sufficiently independent to be able to self-refuel and maintain a healthy local habitat. Di-verse and distributed food systems, energy and water systems would support a global mosaic of regional economies.

What's hopeful about this vision is that it is already partly here. When we choose to research differently, we find already existing diverse economies of care, provisioning and social and environmental redistribution. There is increased exper-imentation with cooperative enterprise, reciprocity, com-moning, ethical markets and community financing; even capitalist enterprise itself is diversifying with the growth of not-for-profits and total reuse companies. Reading the world around us for economic difference is just one step. Having recognized difference, it is much easier to act to "make a dif-ference" (Latour 2005, 253). We can promote the growth of this densely branching bush of proliferating economic activi-ties. Rodents are our teachers—diversified, flexible and nim-ble. How we face the Anthropocene, how we live together as humans, as multi-species beings, as animate and inanimate inhabitants of our life-giving Earth, might come down to rat cunning.

Figure 2. An edible/aesthetic diverse economy, or J.K. Gibson-Graham's writing retreat provisions. Photograph by Katherine Gibson.

17: LISTENING
RESEARCH AS AN ACT OF MINDFULNESS

KUMI KATO

Listening is a critical practice for allowing our senses to awaken and become receptive to Earth Others (Plumwood's term, 2002). All our senses are interrelated, but listening is the practice which has become central to my research. I offer a personal account of the creation of a listening garden, the centerpiece of which is the Japanese "waterharp" *sui-kin-kutsu*. My specific example concerns my experience of sharing joy, passion and often outrage with a group of people committed to a forest in Tasmania. Many of them are creative thinkers and activists who work to save the forest and to express their love for the beauty of the place. Our waterharp installation in a forest in Tasmania enabled us to share and express some of this love and commitment. Before telling the story, though, I need to discuss some of the Japanese concepts and aesthetics which underlie my perceptions and influence my waterharp practice.

In Japanese the word *kiku*—"to listen" can indicate much more than simply a sound coming to our ears. *Kiku* is an act of "appreciating something with all of our sharpened senses." Appreciating the fragrance of incense and the taste of sake, for example, can be *kiku*; such appreciation normally involves identifying and judging quality and more profoundly is a highly established form of art that utilizes all the senses.

The fragrance and visual clarity of sake, for example, and the drifting of incense smoke or the texture of various spices and leaves are all "listened" to.

Natural phenomena that we may listen to include, for example "frost bell" and "dew resonance." A "frost bell" (*shi-monokan,* 霜の鐘) symbolizes the total silence of an extremely cold night, a night so cold that we can hear the sound of frost forming like the subtle ringing of a bell. The word connotes an image of being in the deep night, with almost painfully cold clear air that enhances the glow of silver-blue stars. Or again, we are at the edge of the dawn and as the day breaks, a subtle light, a "dew resonance" (*tamayura,* 玉響) may be felt. A "dew resonance" literally means a drop of dew on a leaf that forms in the early morning before sunrise, which will be gone by the time the full daylight begins. The dewdrops, only visible in a subtle dawn light, look like precious stones that may touch each other ever so slightly as they disappear. That resonance symbolizes the transient fragility of things passing, in both human and non-human worlds; it holds and expresses a moment of serenity and ephemeral beauty.

A particularly beautiful example of *kiku* involves lotus flowers. One early morning in early summer, during the early Showa period (1925–1989), a group of people gathered near a pond in a central parkland to listen to the sound of a lotus flower opening. As the sonic frequency of the lotus opening (9-16Hz) is much lower than the normal frequency range of 20Hz to 20,000Hz of human capability, it was clearly impossible for humans to actually hear the sound of the blooming. The gathering however was attended by people, who brought to the event their aesthetic appreciation of the lotus flower's subtle color, the softness of the petals, the reflection on the water, the pleasant experience of the early morning breeze and the fact that the flower opens only for four days. In fact, it opens only for a few hours in the early morning, and on the fourth day the petals fall, ending the flower's short life. Lotus flowers in Buddhism are regarded as sacred, and the sweet fragrance wafting in the gentle breeze is considered heavenly.

Figure 1. Winter dawn. Photograph by Simon Wearne.

Deep attentive listening is an act of honoring—honoring the other, who speaks to us, telling the stories of their being in various voices and sounds. Listening is a humbling act, for the ephemeral and transient quality of the sound demands a degree of attention and focus. Especially when the sound is subtle, irregular or unpredictable, we are called to focus. We stay still, stop other activities or close our eyes to listen, suppressing other senses, so that our undivided attention can be given to the sound. Listening, in this sense, is a dedication of our attention to the sound and its source, honoring the time and space of its existence. With an attentive respect to the process, we learn that sounds expand freely and eventually dissolve into space. Such mindful and sensuous listening allows the emergence of a world normally invisible to us.

The concept of "soundscape" (Schafer 1977) extends to include invisible sounds that touch our senses and feelings. *Sui-kin-kutsu* is one device that creates the possibility for just such a soundscape. *Sui-kin-kutsu* (水琴窟)—literally, water, harp, cave—is made by burying an inverted terracotta pot (40~60cm in depth) underground with a small hole at the top (three centimeters in diameter). It is devised so that water pools about ten centimeters at the bottom, leaving the rest hollow. Slow dripping water splashes in the water pool and creates a harp-like resonance. Multiple random drops of water create melodic tunes. The sounds can be tuned by varying the depth of the water; equally, though, the humidity, type of soil and shape of the pot produce different kinds of sounds, and the season, the weather on any given day, and also the degree of attentiveness of the listener all have a bearing on the sound. A *sui-kin-kutsu* garden is a conceptually and physically creative space where the surrounding natural elements "play sounds and sing" for an attentive deep listener.

I have been involved in five *sui-kin-kutsu* garden projects created with a clear intention to facilitate mindful and sensuous listening. The intended listening might relate to an issue of forest conservation, water conservation, Indigenous land history or values associated with cetacean, all of which have degrees of socio-political conflict that permeate and affect communities and individuals. For example, our first *sui-kin-kutsu* project was initiated as a collaboration between a group of Japanese students and members of a conservation group "Friends of the Blue Tier" who believed in the values of the forests other than as a commodity resource (Kato 2007). The waterharp was installed in the forest itself as a celebration of the beauty of the place, and of the trust and friendship that developed among the students and conservationists who worked together.

Other garden projects I was involved in include an installation in a parkland in central Brisbane, another in a seaside water education park in Harvey Bay, central Qld, and others in the fishing town of Taiji, Japan and its sister-town Broome, Western Australia (the Taiji-Broome project was initiated by an Australian scholar, Simon Wearne). Each of them is in a sense an interactive "public art" that pays respect to both the natural and cultural space in the local environment. In Australia, this means that paying respect and seeking formal permission from the traditional owners of the land was the first step of the project, and each installation was endorsed and celebrated by the traditional owners of the land—the Blue Tier forest by the Meenamatta People, Brisbane Parkland by the Turrbul people, the seaside water education park in Harvey Bay by the Badjera People and the Broome project by the Yawuru people.

It is an honor to have been permitted to develop installations in these places, to add another layer of cultural story to the land, and to create a space for people to listen. Listening to the waterharp may help to "open ears", as Murray Shafer says, preparing listeners for a much deeper and more intensive use of all the senses. Almost magically, what emerges are soundscapes that are totally unique to each listener.

Pauline Oliveros defined deep listening as "a philosophy and practice that cultivates appreciation of sounds on a heightened level, expanding the potential for connection and interaction with one's environment, technology and performance with others in music and related arts" (Oliveros 2005). With deep listening (also a term and philosophy developed by the Deep Listening Institute[1]), what emerges around us is a soundscape in the sense that Feld defines. In his research, he has come to understand soundscapes as:

> not just physical exteriors, spatially surrounding or apart from human activity, but . . . perceived and interpreted by human actors who attend to them as a way of making their place in and through the world. Soundscapes are invested with significance by those whose bodies and lives resonate with them in social time and space. Like landscapes, they are as much conceptual as physical phenomena, as much cultural constructs as materials ones. (Feld 2003, 226)

Being in a soundscape is clearly a process of engagement with an environment that continually changes; such an engagement involves our behavior, state of mind and senses, as well as the surrounding world. Listening that is immersed in a soundscape forms (even if only momentarily) a dialogical connection with land and place. This is a deep reciprocity of listening, and as Feld describes:

> an embodied dialogue of inner and outer sounding and

---

[1] Deep Listening Institute: http://deeplistening.org/site/content/home.

> resounding built from the historicization of experience. The ongoing dialogue of self and self, self and other, of their interplay in action and reaction, are thus constantly sited at the sense of sound, absorbed and reflected, given and taken in constant exchange. (Feld 2003, 184)

The dialogical nature of the relationship formed with a place is also central to the philosophy of Val Plumwood, who proposed that we need a "two-way and two-place" relationship, in which "you belong to the land as much as the land belongs to you" and which contains "a certain kind of communicative capacity that recognizes the elements that supports our lives" (Plumwood 2002, 220). Such connection, she suggests, is the spirituality that is an essential element in developing a better earth ethics and culture (229–230).

What emerges through deep listening is a broad and embracing mode of engaging with the world using sound as an agent. Through such awareness, listening becomes an act of mindfulness and compassion—for both human and non-human, animate and inanimate, tangible and intangible.

In sum, the humble act of listening involves sensing invisible connections; this is what guides me in my research. I feel an immense sense of privilege for having this opportunity to gain a deeper understanding of being in this world. Tim Flannery, in discussing his latest book *Here on Earth: An Argument for Hope*, states that the reductionist science he has practiced all his life is good at answering small questions, but not helpful in understanding the complex systems of the water, food, climate, and biodiversity crises we now face.[2] Flannery advocates a new model world based on love, empathy and trust and cooperation. Belief in humanity's fundamental capability for change is enlightening, especially if it is based on its capacity to love and empathize. A humble act of listening can become the powerful beginning of connection in all its complexity and depth.

---

[2] See Fran Kelley's interview with Tim Flannery on ABC Radio's *RN Breakfast* here: http://www.abc.net.au/radionational/programs/break fast/videotim-flannery---here-on-earth/2957598.

18: Deep Mapping Connections to Country

Margaret J. Somerville

Maps both represent and shape the places of our world. The practice of deep mapping involves Indigenous and non-Indigenous people working together to create processes by which to re-imagine relationships to place. This practice began during long term partnership research with Aboriginal communities in settled Australia in which together we sought ways to represent contemporary Aboriginal place knowledges that challenge how relationships to land, or the environment, are generally understood and enacted. The maps represent both past relationships and contemporary stories about how places have come to be as they are. They re-inscribe stories of deep time, a time when the earth and all its creatures were made, but a time that exists in the present as well as the geological past. Each time a story is told or represented through deep mapping the deep time stories of creation are re-enacted. Deep mapping becomes a way that one's responsibilities to care for country continue into the present and can be shared by all who inhabit that place. These maps guide us towards an ethical future of living in the Anthropocene.

The practice of deep mapping developed out of the place story research method in which oral stories about place are recorded and at the same time marked on a map of the landscape (Somerville and Perkins 2010). In the deep mapping process a road map of country is used during the storytelling to mark the places on the map where the story events happened. The story is digitally recorded and transcribed and key story excerpts and place names are identified. The roads and towns are then removed from the map using Photoshop software, and the place names and story text are inserted, in a symbolic reversal of the processes of colonization. These maps are then used for further research and storytelling, and as community owned resources for cultural teaching. The stories produced in this way can be story events of everyday life, of past histories and memories, and of dreaming or creation stories. These are often the same places, where creation stories, histories and daily living stories occur simultaneously in a place in layers over deep time. We use the descriptor "deep" to indicate this layering over geological time with each layer visible in the present and shaping contemporary places and relationships.

Through deep mapping special place stories that have been erased, or rendered silent and invisible, are reconnected to the land. The storylines of the creation ancestors recorded by early linguists become songlines again through reconnecting the events in the story to their places in the landscape. In traditional times, at each special place where an event in the creation story happened, the place and all its creatures were sung into being in ceremony. These were places of deep learning. Where language and stories have been disconnected from country, detailed and intense language work is at the heart of deep mapping. By mapping the events in the recorded language stories back onto the landscape, deep mapping becomes another process for singing the country. Each time the story is told through sharing such a map and its stories, the places, the language, and the stories are remade.

A walking story in Gumbaynggirr country on the mid north coast of New South Wales, for example, mapped out part of the storyline of the creation ancestor Birrugan. Birrugan's storyline creates the places, people and connections in the country of the Nambucca River estuary. I worked with

Martin, a Gumbaynggirr Elder who recorded his memories of walking with extended family members from Bowraville Mission to visit other relatives on Stuart Island in the Nambucca River estuary. To map Martin's walking story is to enter a world of knowing country through walking. It begins as a journey from one place to the other, and like all good travelling stories departs in the middle with a digression about his totemic cobra place connections ("I'm a Guggurr man"), revealing the intricacies of walking knowledge and intersecting trails.

Martin oriented himself to the road map by finding the river and then the different places along the way. Place is infinitely detailed as he marks Wirriimbi Island, a white-owned farming property they walked through, a little creek that flows into the river, and a flat where they met up with the women and children after the boys had been taken aside by the older men. The boys (and the girls too, but their story is not Martin's) were already learning special knowledge as they walked with the Old People. They learned to hunt, spear, and collect wild fruits: "The Uncles of me, they taught me to do the spearing—how to do things." As the walking proceeds, stories are told about the past and the present as story places open up along the way. We pass an area that Martin describes as a "no-go zone" because it is marked by a sacred "diamond tree": "maybe there was a massacre site there." Stories of linking trails contain symbolic and intricate, deeply coded references to other places and place knowledge.

The mapping of Martin's walking trail gives us insight into the basis of the songlines that criss-cross Gumbaynggirr country. A songline is a walking trail that links the story events, the path that the creation ancestors followed as they did the same, walking through country, collecting food, and living out the events in their lives that are marked forever in the landscape. When grids of roads and buildings transform the outward appearance of the place, the story remains as a reminder of deep connection. Each of the special places along a storyline has a song that evokes all the other aspects of the ceremony. Songs are connected in a songline through the linking trails.

The songlines that followed the linking trails are no longer walked, but were taught as stories by the Old People: "because we never got the chance to do all the old travelling ways." These stories were recorded in language when the old initiated men sought linguists to record their stories in times of turbulence and change. Significantly the Old People also recorded some of the songs that embodied the highest level of ceremonial knowledge of the special places on the linking trails. In deep mapping with cultural knowledge holders and language workers from Murrbay Language and Culture Centre, we mapped layers of place stories through time. We mapped storylines of the places where Gumbaynggirr people live now, where they lived in the historic past, and the deep time creation stories of the ancestors.

Figure 1. Baby possum skin cloak, 2008. Artist Treahna Hamm. Photograph by Margaret Somerville.

These learnings were applied in a later project, opening up our research processes to the emergence of new forms. We became more creative and experimental with the kinds of maps we produced. In a project about water in a dry land, Aboriginal artists from different language groups along the waterways of the vast Murray-Darling river system created maps of country with their artworks. Treahna Hamm, a Yorta Yorta artist from the Murray River made maps on possum skin cloaks. Treahna had been involved in several major projects of re-creating possum skin cloaks with communities across Victoria (Reynolds et al. 2005). In the cold country of southern Australia possum skin cloaks were traditionally inscribed with the symbols of identity in country and used in ceremony as well as everyday life. They were so precious that they were buried with their owners and only two remained in museums in Victoria. Treahna made drawings of the symbols on the cloak that came from her Yorta Yorta country on the Murray River. Re-inventing possum skin cloaks as a contemporary place-making practice, she made a full length possum skin cloak to map the story of Biame, the great creation figure for the Murray River:

> Biame sent the old woman
> down from the alps
> she walked along
> with her stick
> and two camp dogs
> and created a line in the sand,
> and the camp dogs followed
> Biame then sent
> the serpent to follow her
> and he followed the line
> that she dug in the sand
> which made the bed
> of the river
> he sent down the rain,
> that filled up the Murray.
> She walked right down the river
> to the mouth of the Murray
> and she fell asleep
> in a cave down there
> you can hear the sea
> it's the old woman
> singing in her sleep. (Somerville 2013, 164)

Our team of Aboriginal and non-Aboriginal researchers

recorded our conversations as our sense of ourselves and our possibilities for re-making our relationship to country emerged in this work.

> Imagine the river
> without a map
> having it in your head
> that's how people
> found their way
> if they got lost
> the little ones
> would start
> with a small cloak
> as they got older
> they could come along
> with it on
> just throw it down
> and talk with the mob
> this is my country.
> Where I come from.
> You could wear it
> as a cloak
> and use it as a map
> together. (Somerville 2013, 169)

Deep mapping is a process whereby globally we can learn together to listen to the stories of the land and to tell its stories in different ways. Those ways involve us in recognizing the imperative to create new connections through bringing age-old stories and knowledges into a contemporary present.

19: THE HUMAN CONDITION IN THE ANTHROPOCENE

ANNA YEATMAN

Hannah Arendt is a political philosopher who seems to have anticipated our current moment; one where it seems increasingly likely that humanly made processes may undermine the integrity of the living system that is "life on earth" and threaten its collapse. At the risk of offering too potted a summary of what was a complex series of meditations developed over the course of her career as a political philosopher, I want to suggest the nature of her prescience in regard to what she called "the human condition" and the human desire to reconcile themselves to "reality, that is, try to be at home in the world" (Arendt 1994, 308).

The many insightful issues she addressed boil down to one primary concern—the loss of a sense of reality as given, a sense that underpins the acceptance of a world that we have in common. For Arendt, this amounts to the possibility that the human condition may itself be lost. Here she shares with Judaism a profound conviction that to be human is to be a living creature, an earthly creature, for it is the earth that provides human beings and other living beings "with a habitat in which they can move and breathe without effort and without artifice" (Arendt 1958, 2). In contrast to the Christian disdain of earthly affairs in favor of eternal life, Arendt speaks of "the altogether different teachings of the Hebrews, who always held that life itself is sacred, more sacred than anything else in the world, and that man is the supreme being on earth" (Arendt 1977, 52). The tradition of Judaism was Arendt's to inherit, and I have no doubt at all that the fundamentals of Judaism frame Arendt's thinking in ways of which she had some awareness.

Being alive is the condition of all other human activities, and, indeed, Arendt traces how the "three fundamental human activities" of labor, work, and action, each, in different ways articulate what it means to be alive, and, by the same token, to be mortal. Labor tends to the cyclical organic aspects of being alive; work expresses a human need to build a shared world of things and structures that link generations and, in this way, transcend the mortality of individuals; and action expresses a human capacity for the symbolic articulation of the uniqueness of the individual living being in speech and deeds that bring about a creative rupture with what is given. The human way of being alive both ties humans to other creaturely beings and differentiates humans from them. But being alive, as such, is what these beings have in common, and it indicates a shared dependence on an earthbound existence.

Writing in the 1950s, Arendt is profoundly aware that modern science has little or no respect for this shared earthly nature of humans and animals:

For some time now, a great many scientific endeavors have been directed toward making life also "artificial," toward cutting the last tie through which even man belongs among the children of nature. It is the same desire to escape from imprisonment to the earth that is manifest in the attempt to create life in the test tube, in the desire to mix "frozen germ plasm from people of demonstrated ability under the microscope to produce superior human beings" and "to alter [their] size, shape and function"; and the wish to escape the human condition, I suspect also underlies the hope to extend man's life-span far beyond the hundred-year limit. (Arendt 1958, 2)

It is the desire to escape "human existence as it has been given to man" (Arendt 1958, 7) that is at issue for Arendt, and, as indicated in the following passage that continues the last one cited, she has no doubt that this desire can be realized even if it leads to an end of the human (and the shared creaturely) condition:

> This future man, whom the scientists tell us they will produce in no more than a hundred years, seems to be possessed by a rebellion against human existence as it has been given, a free gift from nowhere (secularly speaking) which he wishes to exchange, as it were, for something he has made himself. There is no reason to doubt our abilities to accomplish such an exchange, just as there is no reason to doubt our present ability to destroy all organic life on earth. (Arendt 1958, 2–3)

I have thought a good deal about Arendt's diagnosis of modern times. I cannot fault it. It hinges, it seems to me, on the question of whether we are able to know and value what it means to be alive, and, it follows, to be in the "live company" (Alvarez 1992) of other creaturely beings. Knowing and valuing what it means to be alive is not a matter of intellection. It is thus I find it impossible in the academic classroom to reason why we should know and value what it means to be alive. Rather it is a matter of embodied awareness, an awareness that may lead us to question what it is we think we, moderns, know, and to revalue what it is we have dismissed by way of tradition and religion.

In so saying, I am not suggesting that we should throw out the valuable aspects of modern skepticism, not least of these being the freedom to doubt, but I am saying that, if we value what it means to be alive, we must place our skepticism in service to being alive, and to its distinctive joys and sorrows. If we wish to value, just as Arendt did, the creative force of action in its power to call into question the given, we have also somehow to limit how far we identify with the freedom of action. This, of course, we may find impossible.

20: DIALOGUE

DEBORAH BIRD ROSE

The term "dialogue" has joined a class of weasel words used to pretend that an exchange is taking place when actually the will of one party is being imposed on others. This is a fact to be resisted, for dialogue is an excellent word denoting inter-subjective exchanges of ideas, stories, empathy, imagery, and much more. Because of its current misuse, the project of re-claiming the term requires a clear analysis of monologue. Monologue, once it is understood, cannot be confused with dialogue. The distinction rests primarily on the power struc-ture between the parties to the event.

Critical theory and philosophical analysis have shown Western thought and action to be subtended by a set of bina-ries that, as has been discussed, demarcate categories that are ordered by hierarchy and privilege. The critical intervention in feminist analysis, in particular, is to show that while the binary looks like it could be a relationship between two op-posites, it is actually a form of power that obliterates the "others." Luce Irigaray (1985), for example, shows that the defining feature of woman under phallocentric thought is that she is not man. Stripped of much cultural elaboration, this structure articulates a power relation such that one side of the binary is a site of presence and action, while the other side is a site of absence and passivity. Defined as all that it is not, the absent, or passive pole, is inevitably the recipient of monological practice; within the logic of the binary, it could not be anything else.

I have written elsewhere that a crucial feature of this structure is that the other never gets to talk back on its own terms (Rose 2004, 19–21). Power lies in the ability not to hear what is being said, not to experience the consequences of one's actions, but rather to go one's own self-centric and in-sulated way. The communication is all one way, and the pole of power sustains its privilege by refusing any feedback that would cause it to open itself to dialogue.

The image of bipolarity therefore masks what is, in effect, only a pole of self/power. The self sets itself within a hall of mirrors, sees itself endlessly reflected as if the world were indeed a reflection of the self, talks endlessly to itself, and, not surprisingly, finds constant affirmation of itself and its power. This is monologue masquerading as conversation, masturbation purporting to be productive interaction; it is a narcissism so profound that it claims to find a universal knowledge when in fact its violent erasures are universalising its own singular and powerful isolation. This is not to say that monologue itself lacks debate and conflict, but more deeply that it is self-totalising in only including what it can accommodate within its own narrative, and by insisting that others, if they appear at all, appear as they are construed by that monological narrative.

This brief critical analysis of monologue demonstrates not only how dialogue must differ, but also why we need dia-logue. The monological view of the world rests on a huge error. Actually, the world is rich in life, and living beings have their own meanings, stories, ideas, and desires. Dialogue is a method for opening conversations so that they are inclu-sive and responsive. It is thus a practice founded in an ethics of intersubjectivity.

Initially, my interest in dialogue arose from conditions of life in settler societies; I was seeking an ethics arising out of my own traditions that would help me find a ground from which descendants of settlers and descendants of Indigenous people might initiate a conversation. From the point of view of a descendant of settlers, my questions concerned the conditions that might precede any effort to engage in a conversation. I have drawn on the work of the philosopher Emil Fackenheim because he asks questions about dialogue between Jews and Germans after the Nazi holocaust. Without diminishing the potency and urgency of his particular context, it is, I believe, possible to take his work into other contexts of harm.

Fackenheim ([1982] 1994, 129) draws on the work of Franz Rosenzweig to articulate two main precepts for structuring the ground for ethical dialogue. The first is that dialogue begins where one is, and thus is always situated; the second is that dialogue is open, and thus that the outcome is not known in advance. Our situatedness involves both our membership in the species that is responsible for so much harm, and our embodied, emplaced existence within the social and ecological domains of our lives. To be situated requires us to have knowledge of our place within our ecological contexts, and this requirement poses a problem for us because so much of the harm happens either at a distance from us, or in contexts that we are not well trained to see and understand. In Australia, settler-descendants are situated in damaged places; we bear the burden of the violent history of conquest that has resulted in damage, loss, degradation, and extinctions that amount to ecocide. The brunt of all this wounding has primarily been borne by others; a fair understanding situates us in the midst of damaged lives and damaged places. These are harsh situations, and as I have argued elsewhere, ethical dialogue requires that we acknowledge and understand our particular and harshly situated presence (Rose 2004).

This paradigm for dialogue across chasms of radical harm is especially appropriate for our anthropogenic moment, as we seek to rework our relationships with the living world. Any conversations we humans may wish to start up concerning the living world, our place in it and our responsibilities toward it must bear the knowledge of the terrible harm we have done and continue to do. From an ecologically inflected situated perspective, what matters is the living world, which is the only context within which all of us living creatures are born, live and die. What lies between us and others, are the invasions, the dominations, the deaths and extinctions. Before we lose heart, however, we must also consider that violence is not the whole story. What lies between us and earth others, or between some of us some of the time, is love, respect, sympathy, and the determination to take care of all that we can in this time of crisis. The possibility of dialogue, and its accomplishment in many contexts, rests in the fact that our situatedness is neither wholly destructive nor wholly beneficial. The multi-species, multi-sited entanglements within which all life is lived give us grounds for action.

The concept of openness may sound obvious, but it is equally challenging. Openness is risky because one does not know the outcome. To be open is to hold one's self available to others: one takes risks and becomes vulnerable. But this is also a fertile stance: one's own ground can become destabilised. In open dialogue one holds one's self available to be surprised, to be challenged, and to be changed. Ethical openness challenges us because it contains a contradictory set of injunctions. On the one hand openness is unlimited, since one always wants to try to understand others, and to listen with an open mind. On the other hand, openness has limits: an ethical position does not remain open to assisting violence or to sustaining the silences that oppress. Openness, in brief, is unlimited in its even-handedness, but at the same time is counterbalanced by commitment to flourishing biosocial conviviality.

Dialogue that seeks to alter the conditions which are the cause of so much harm faces an interesting paradox. If there is no vision to guide our action, we run the risk of remaining ineffective, and will have difficulty interesting any one, even ourselves. On the other hand, if there is a vision to guide our actions, we run the risk of losing the open stance that is a necessary feature of dialogue. It may be that the most constructive visions, that is, those most open to dialogue, relate to practice rather than outcome. Val Plumwood was, at the time of her death, working to articulate just such an account of human and nonhuman sentient life that would be defensible philosophically and that could engage dialogically with Indigenous peoples' animism. The term she used was "philosophical animism," and in her words, this project "opens the door to a world in which we can begin to negotiate life membership of an ecological community of kindred beings" (Plumwood 2009).

Once we start to embrace dialogue, we become ever more aware that monologue stifles knowledge of connection and disables the possibilities whereby "self" finds its own meaning and purpose through entangled encounters and responsibilities with "others." The great philosopher of intersubjective ethics, Emmanuel Levinas, writes, "For an ethical sensibility—confirming itself in the inhumanity of our time, against this inhumanity—the justification of the neighbor's pain is certainly the source of all immorality" (Levinas 1988, 163). One of the great tasks before us is to include all of the living world within the domain of "neighbors," and a great consequence of doing so is that we embrace noisy and unruly processes capable of finding dialogue not only with other people but equally with the world itself. Bearing the burden of our histories of harm, and going gently into encounters that are both situated and open, we shake our capacity for connection loose from the bondage of monologue. Only then will we be able to start the work of becoming human in connection with others, negotiating forms of neighborly kinship in the on-going project of life.

21: Walking as Respectful Wayfinding in an Uncertain Age

Lesley Instone

Figure 1. Photograph by Lesley Instone.

In 2010 I made a short trip to the Isle of Lewis in the Outer Hebrides. My main impetus was to visit the ancient standing stones at Calanais as well as experience, however briefly and vicariously, other worlds, lives and landscapes. Regardless that I had only a couple of days on the island, I decided to catch the local bus and walk to the sights rather than hire a car. I'm sure many readers have made similar choices and experienced the delights of being on foot in an unfamiliar place. Instead of the ordinary, regular, enclosed, plastic world of automobility, I was greeted by smells, animals, uneven surfaces, twisting paths, sheep, dogs, farmers, wind, sun, and more. My intention is not to romanticize walking, nor to suggest a singular notion of walking. How I walk, what I look at, and my practices of movement and thinking are all shaped by historically contingent cultural practices of looking and moving that are familiar to those with a European cultural heritage. Acknowledging this is to understand that walking is as cultural as it is embodied, and that there are many ways to walk, many ways of seeing and knowing (Solnit 2000; Ingold 2000; Amato 2004). What I do want to emphasize is the interrelation between body, knowing, place and feeling. In many ways the random and impromptu qualities of walking engender a kind of openness to surprises and chance encounters that provoke affective ways of knowing (Solnit 2000, 11). The intermeshing of movement, mind, body, land/scape, ground and atmosphere transport us into a realm of inexpressible, ineffable and fleeting relatings, where we know "the world through the body and the body through the world" (Solnit 2000, 29).

At the end of the day, my sore legs and tired feet reminded me of a gently undulating topography of peat bogs, paddocks, craggy cliffs and scattered settlements. Alongside contemporary lives, on Lewis it is possible to see the remnants of worlds past and those passing. As I walk this landscape I'm reminded of the contingencies of space, time and power. Lewis, once a center of power, is now considered remote and marginal. Its past is revealed on a day's walk where one can go from the Bronze Age standing stones to an Iron Age broch and finish up at recently repaired "blackhouses" belonging to a mode of living more recently gone. Walking slows you down, time passes differently and mind and body are merged in the effort to cover ground and take in the surroundings. That is, every step embodies time as well as space, each step meshing things past and those to come in an ongoing process, each step participating in the making of worlds and in the process, knitting together responsibility for past, present and future.

On Lewis I experienced what many walkers encounter—a different pace and perspective, a different way of seeing and feeling (Wylie 2005; Phillips 2005). These qualities add up to understanding walking as a kind of knowledge-making—in that how I moved through the land/scape and among the people, animals and townships of Lewis was constitutive of how and what I learned about the place and related to it, as well as how the place shaped my mind and body as I moved in and through it. David Turnbull gives insight into the relationship between movement and knowledge in his consideration of another set of stones—the Maltese Megaliths. Turnbull (2002) describes the megaliths as "theatres of knowledge" in order to emphasize the co-production of cognitive, material and social worlds, so that "knowledge, artifacts and human agents work together to produce our lived lives in the world" (125). This performative understanding of space and knowledge highlights the complex processes through which worlds are always relational achievements and perpetually "in-the-making," never fixed or pre-given. We enact structures and landscapes at the same time that material worlds— be they standing stones or concrete walkways or a track through the bush—may direct, facilitate or constrain movement thereby shaping human experience and encounters with others (135). Modes of movement, such as walking, therefore, can help us not just experience things differently but can help to build different knowledges. This is knowledge forged in the spirit of "wayfinding"—an always unfinished, rhythmic, open and creative mode of being-in-the-world that embraces the twin entanglements of movement and being moved (Dening 2008; Ingold 2000; Lee and Ingold 2006).

Way-finding, or what Ingold refers to as wayfaring, is a

sort of wandering line, or more precisely, a rich meshwork that weaves and textures "the trails *along* which life is lived" (Ingold 2007, 81, italics in original). It endorses a performance of respectfulness towards otherness that invokes "myriad expressions" of difference and a sense of wonder that moves us so that "no knowledge, no image is stilled in either time or space" (Dening 2008, 147–148).

The story I've told about walking on Lewis features the common western trope of the lone human figure, walking and thinking in harmonious relation with the world around (Solnit 2000). But this is a misleading image that tempts us into thinking that we humans are the main actors, and that thinking alone (in both senses) can shape better worlds. The human-centeredness of much writing on walking was brought home to me by Lyanda Lynn Haupt's book *Crow Planet* (2009), a charming and perceptive look at the interconnectedness of humans and others in the ordinary spaces and places of suburban life. Whether we realize it or not, whenever we walk we are walking alongside multiple others, human and nonhuman, and how we move is likewise not only a human achievement, but shaped by the more-than-human worlds through which we step. Like us, Haupt points out, crows are bipedal, they're intelligent, adaptable, use technology, and spend much of their time walking. Crows are "good to think with" because they're not rare, not universally liked or appreciated, and not cute. Crows therefore challenge us to think in different ways about our relations to more-than-human worlds and challenge us to walk in more considered, open and tolerant ways, ways inclusive of difficult, as well as pleasant, others.[1] Many of us have experience of walking alongside canine companions, and will know how this "humanimal" encounter can stretch our perceptions to smellscapes, different styles of directionality, as well as the enhanced sociality of dog walking for both humans and dogs. Dogs defy our desire for visuality and linearity. Likewise, crows as undomesticated co-walkers, unsettle our habits of

---

[1] See also van Dooren's (2011b) work on vultures.

being and challenge us further to make a place for unchosen and uncomfortable others. That's why Haupt says that crows "are so entirely relevant to our place on a changing earth, [as] they help us to 'reimagine a different future'" (202). For instance, walking-with crows means facing up to the wasteful consumer-driven and careless lifestyles that feed the piles of rubbish and roadkill on which crows thrive and multiply (202).

Thinking about walking-with crows brings a more-than-human resonance to practices of movement. "Walking-with" highlights mutuality, respect, plurality, and engenders a respectful "being-for" in the sense of kindling practices of movement and engagement that not only acknowledge the place and presence of others, but that contribute to, and allow space for, their flourishing (Howitt 2011). Walking-with others involves our hearts as well as heads, legs, guts, and minds. It combines rational and more-than-rational knowing. It is a kind of engagement with the world and otherness that can change our step and take us down unexpected pathways.

At first glance, "walking" and the "Anthropocene" do not seem to go easily together. After all, walking is slow, fragile, unreliable—it's hardly a mode of movement suited to grappling with the pressing issues the Anthropocene heralds. Surely we don't have time to dawdle in the face of the urgent politics of global change? But in another sense, walking might be exactly what we need. The slow, engaged and engaging attributes of walking might indeed help to enhance our connectedness with the world in embodied and creative ways. The mode of walking and wayfinding appropriate to the Anthropocene isn't a headlong rush to get somewhere "better" or the conceit of thinking that we have the answers. Rather it's a studied movement of the here and now, a fragmentary, wandering, lively, embodied and relational process. A respectful movement that puts emphasis on sensory, contingent and fragile encounters conjured through making our way, alongside others through time and space, here and now. My experience on the Isle of Lewis brought to life for me how the strands of past walkers, the movement of all manner of non-humans (organic or otherwise), our choices of wayfinding in the present, all tangle together to constitute world, body and the particular places we inhabit.

To me, notions of wayfinding and respectful walking-with are useful ways to think about how to proceed in times of uncertainty, when there's no singular right way, and where we don't know quite where we're headed. The Anthropocene confronts us with an uncertain and unknown future where to follow conventional paths would be to amplify current problems. Wayfinding as an experimental, nonlinear mode of movement helps us meet the challenge of unknowable futures in a changing world. Wayfinding can be playful, lively, and rhizomatic, such that it can accommodate ambiguity, diversity and accountability. With walking, each step poses the possibility of an alternative, each step is a becoming, a journey not an end point (Phillips 2005, 509). In this way, wayfinding and walking-with are not just about movement, communication and knowing, but about making some worlds and not others.

Walking can attune us differently to the world but offers no universal prescription. And, of course, walking, the choice to walk and the freedom to be able to walk, is a privilege not available to all. A privilege not to be squandered or taken lightly. At best it's a generative practice of risking ourselves and risking new relations, rather than falling back on sedimented habits and well-worn paths. The *Manifesto for Living in the Anthropocene* advocates an experimental stance, and you might like to try out some walking experiments of your own. You might like to try some seriously playful walking-with crows, lizards, dingoes, as well as refugees, unfamiliar people, children, your neighbor, and the many others who together make our worlds. You might like to practice co-motion to cause a little commotion, way-find towards practices that diminish waste and consumption and enhance the flourishing of others. Who knows where they will take you and what you will find out along the way, but respectful walking-with and a spirit of wayfinding will, I believe, take you a long way.

REFERENCES

Abram, David. 1997. *The Spell of the Sensuous: Perception and Language in a More-than-Human World*. New York: Vintage.

Alvarez, Anne. 1992. *Live Company: Psychoanalytic Psychotherapy with Autistic, Borderline, Deprived and Abused Children*. London: Routledge.

Amato, Joseph A. 2004. *On Foot: A History of Walking*. New York: New York University Press.

Andrews, Peter. 2006. *Back from the Brink: How Australia's Landscape Can Be Saved*. Sydney: ABC Books.

APCRI [Assoc. for Prevention and Control of Rabies in India]. 2004. *Assessing the Burden of Rabies in India—WHO Sponsored National Multi-centric Rabies Survey 2003. Bangalore: Association for the Prevention and Control of Rabies in India*: http://rabies.org.in/rabies/wp-content/uploads/2009/11/whosurvey.pdf.

Arendt, Hannah. 1958. *The Human Condition*. Chicago: University of Chicago Press.

Arendt, Hannah. 1977. "The Concept of History Ancient and Modern." In Hannah Arendt, *Between Past and Future*, 41–91. New York: Penguin Books.

Arendt, Hannah. 1994. "Understanding in Politics." In Hannah Arendt, *Essays in Understanding 1930-1954: For-*

mation, Exile and Totalitarianism, Jerome Kohn (ed), 307–328. New York: Harcourt Brace and Jovanovich.

Bateson, Gregory. [1972] 1973. *Steps to an Ecology of Mind.* London: Granada Publishing Limited/Paladin Books.

Beck, Ulrich. 1992. *Risk Society: Towards a New Modernity*, Mark Ritter (trans). London: Sage.

Beck, Ulrich. 2006. *Cosmopolitan Vision*, Ciaran Cronin (trans). Cambridge: Polity Press.

Bekoff, Marc. 2002. *Minding Animals: Awareness, Emotions, and Heart.* Oxford: Oxford University Press.

Bekoff, Marc and Jessica Pierce. 2009. *Wild Justice: The Moral Lives of Animals.* Chicago: University of Chicago Press.

Benyus, Janine. 2002. *Biomimicry: Innovation Inspired by Nature.* New York: Perennial Publishers.

Blundell, Sally. 2006. "The Thinking Machine." *New Zealand Listener*, July 29: http://www.listener.co.nz/culture/the-thinking-machine/.

Booth, Carol, Kerryn Parry-Jones, Nicola Beynon, Nancy Pallin, and Bob James. 2008. *Why NSW Should Ban the Shooting of Flying Foxes.* Report by Humane Society International Australia: http://hsi.org.au/editor/assets/FFre portDec08.pdf.

Botkin, Daniel. 1992. *Discordant Harmonies: A New Ecology for the Twenty-First Century.* Oxford: Oxford University Press.

Callon, Michel. 2007. "What Does It Mean to Say that Economics Is Performative?" In *Do Economists Make Markets: On the Performativity of Economics,* Donald MacKenzie, Fabian Muniesa, and Lucia Sui (eds), 311–357. Princeton: Princeton University Press.

Cameron, Jenny and J.K. Gibson-Graham. 2003. "Feminising the Economy: Metaphors, Strategies, Politics." *Gender, Place and Culture* 10(2): 145–157.

Chakrabarty, Dipesh. 2009. "The Climate of History: Four Theses." *Critical Inquiry* 35(2): 197–222.

Conradson, David. 2003. "Spaces of Care in the City: The Place of a Community Drop-in Centre." *Social and Cultural Geography* 4(4): 507–525.

Dening, Greg. 2008. "Respectfulness as a Performance Art: Way-finding." *Postcolonial Studies* 11(2): 145–155.

Dumanoski, Dianne. 2009. *The End of the Long Summer: Why We Must Remake Our Civilization to Survive on a Volatile Earth.* New York: Crown Publishers.

Eastley, Tony. 2009. "Muswellbrook Miner Speaks out Against Coal Industry." *Three Men in a Car, Hunter Roadshow,* AM Program. ABC Radio, August 12: http://www.abc.net.au/am/content/2009/s2653161.htm.

Eby, P. 1991. "Seasonal Movements of Grey-headed Flying-foxes, *Pteropus poliocephalus* (Chiroptera: Pteropodidae), from two maternity camps in northern New South Wales." *Wildlife Research* 18(5): 547–559.

Eno, Brian. 2000. "The Big Here and the Long Now." *The Long Now*: http://www.longnow.org/essays/big-here-long-now/.

Fackenheim, Emil. [1982] 1994. *To Mend the World, Foundations of Post-Holocaust Jewish Thought.* Bloomington: Indiana University Press.

Feld, Steven. 2003. "Rainforest Acoustemology." In *The Auditory Culture Reader,* Michael Bull and Les Back (eds), 223–239. Oxford: Berg Publishers.

Fincher, Ruth and Kurt Iveson. 2008. *Planning and Diversity in the City: Redistribution, Recognition and Encounter.* London: Palgrave Macmillan.

Fincher, Ruth, Paul Carter, Paolo Tombesi, Kate Shaw, and Andrew Martel. 2009. *Transnational and Temporary: Students, Community and Place-making in Central Melbourne* (Final Report). University of Melbourne: http://www.transnationalandtemporary.com.au.

Flannery, Tim. 2010. *Here on Earth: an Argument for Hope.* Melbourne: The Text Publishing.

Foucault, Michel. 1980. *Power/Knowledge: Selected Interviews and Other Writings, 1972–1977,* Colin Gordon (ed). New York: Pantheon.

Fyfe, Melissa. 2005. "Rising Temperatures Could Spell Doom for Many of the Delicate Creatures in Queensland's Wet Tropical Rainforest." *The Age* (Melbourne), November 16:

http://www.jcu.edu.au/rainforest/releases/the_rainforest.pdf.

Gibson-Graham, J.K. 1996. *The End of Capitalism (As We Knew It): A Feminist Critique of Political Economy.* Oxford: Blackwell Publishers.

Gibson-Graham, J.K. 2006. *A Postcapitalist Politics.* Minneapolis: University of Minnesota Press.

Gibson-Graham, J.K. and Gerda Roelvink. 2010. "An Economic Ethics for the Anthropocene." *Antipode* 41(1): 320–346.

Gleeson, Brendan. 2010. *Lifeboat Cities.* Sydney: UNSW Press.

Goldney, David. 2005. "Interview with Land Ecologist Professor David Goldney." *Australian Story,* ABC Radio, June 6: http://www.abc.net.au/austory/content/2005/s1384171.htm.

Gould, Stephen Jay. 1991. *Bully for Brontosaurus: Reflections in Natural History.* New York: W.W. Norton.

Graham, Mary. 2008. "Some Thoughts on the Philosophical Underpinnings of Aboriginal Worldviews." *Australian Humanities Review* 45: 181–194.

Griffiths, Tom. 2007. "The Humanities and an Environmentally Sustainable Australia." Eco-humanities Corner: *Australian Humanities Review* 43: http://www.australianhumanities review.org/archive/Issue-December2007/EcoHumanities/EcoGriffiths.html.

Grinde, Donald and Bruce Johansen. 1995. *Ecocide of Native America: Environmental Destruction of Indian Lands and Peoples.* Santa Fe: Clear Light Publishers.

Gronda, Hellene. 2005. *Dance with the Body You Have: Body Awareness Practices and/as Deconstruction.* PhD thesis, Monash University, Australia.

Hall, Leslie, and Greg Richards. 2000. *Flying Foxes: Fruit and Blossom Bats of Australia.* Sydney: UNSW Press.

Haraway, Donna. 2008. *When Species Meet.* Minneapolis: University of Minnesota Press.

Harding, Stephan. 2006. *Animate Earth: Science, Intuition and Gaia.* Foxhole, UK: Green Books Ltd.

Hatley, James. 2000. *Suffering Witness: The Quandary of Re-*

sponsibility after the Irreparable. New York: State University of New York Press.

Haupt, Lyanda Lynn. 2009. *Crow Planet: Essential Wisdom from the Urban Wilderness.* New York: Little, Brown and Company.

Hird, Myra. 2009. *The Origins of Sociable Life: Evolution after Science Studies.* Houndmills, UK: Palgrave Macmillan.

Hird, Myra. 2010. "Coevolution, Symbiosis and Sociology." *Ecological Economics* 69(4): 737–742.

Holmgren, David. 2002. *Permaculture: Principles and Pathways beyond Sustainability.* Hepburn, Victoria: Holmgren Design Services.

Howitt, Richie. 2011. "Ethics as First Method: Rethinking Ethical Engagement in Intercultural Social Research." Paper presented at IAG [Institute of Australian Geographers] Conference, "Geography on the Edge," University of Wollongong, July 3-6.

Hulme, Mike and Martin Mahony. 2010, "Climate Change: What Do We Know about the IPCC?" *Progress in Physical Geography* 34(5): 705–718.

Ingold Timothy. 2000. *The Perception of the Environment: Essays in Livelihood, Dwelling and Skill.* London: Routledge.

Ingold, Tim. 2007. *Lines: A Brief History.* London: Routledge.

Irigaray, Luce. 1985. *This Sex Which Is Not One,* Catherine Porter (trans). Ithaca: Cornell University Press.

Jacobs, Jane. 2000. *The Nature of Economies.* New York: Vintage Books.

Jullien, Francois. 2002. "Did Philosophers Have to Become Fixated on Truth?" *Critical Inquiry* 28(4): 547–571.

Kato, Kumi. 2007. "Addressing Global Responsibility through Cross-cultural Collaboration." *The Environmentalist* 28(2): 148–154.

Kinnane, Steve. 2002. "Recurring visions of Australindia." In *Country: Visions of Land and People in Western Australia,* Andrea Gaynor, Mathew Trinca and Anna Haebich (eds), 21–31. Perth: Western Australian Museum.

Latour, Bruno. 2004a. *Politics of Nature: How to Bring the*

Sciences into Democracy, Catherine Porter (trans). Cambridge: Harvard University Press.

Latour, Bruno. 2004b. "How to Talk About the Body: The Normative Dimension of Science Studies." *Body & Society* 10: 205–229.

Latour, Bruno. 2005. *Reassembling the Social: An Introduction to Actor-Network-Theory.* Oxford: Oxford University Press.

Lee, Jo, and Tim Ingold. 2006. "Fieldwork on Foot." In *Locating the Field: Space, Place and Context in Anthropology*, Simon Coleman and Peter Collins (eds), 67–85. London: Berg.

Leopold, Aldo. 1949. *A Sand County Almanac.* London: Oxford University Press.

Levinas, Emmanuel. 1988. "The Paradox of Morality: An Interview with Emmanuel Levinas." In *The Provocation of Levinas: Rethinking the Other,* R. Bernasconi and D. Woods (eds), 168–180. London: Routledge.

The Long Now Foundation. n.d. "The 10,000 Year Clock." *The Long Now Foundation*: http://www.longnow.org/clock/.

Lovelock, James. 2000. *Gaia: The Practical Science of Planetary Medicine.* Oxford: Oxford University Press.

Macdonald, David, and M. Karen Laurenson. 2006. "Infectious Disease: Inextricable Linkages Between Human and Ecosystem Health." *Biological Conservation* 131(2): 143–150.

MacDougall, David. 2006. *Corporeal Image: Film, Ethnography, and the Senses.* Princeton: Princeton University Press.

Manning, Paddy. 2009. "Mining Stalwart Sees No Future in Carbon Plan." *Sydney Morning Herald*, April 25: http://www.smh.com.au/business/mining-stalwart-sees-no-future-in-carbon-plan-20090424-ai16.html.

Margulis, Lynn and Dorion Sagan. 1995. *What Is Life?* Berkeley: University of California Press.

Markandya, Anil, Tim Taylor, Alberto Longo, M.N. Murty, S. Murty, and K. Dhavala. "Counting the Cost of Vulture Declines: An Appraisal of the Human Health and Other

Benefits of Vultures in India." *Ecological Economics* 67(2): 194–204.

Martin, Len, and Alan McIlwee. 2002. "The Reproductive Biology and Intrinsic Capacity for Increase of the Grey-Headed Flying-Fox Poliocephalus (Megachiroptera), and the Implications of Culling." In *Managing the Grey-headed Flying-fox as a Threatened Species in NSW,* Peggy Eby and Daniel Lunney (eds), 91–108. Sydney: Royal Zoological Society of New South Wales.

Mathews, Freya. 2011a. "Planet Beehive." *Australian Humanities Review* 50: 159–178.

Mathews, Freya. 2011b. "Towards a Deeper Philosophy of Biomimicry." *Organization and Environment* 24(4): 364–87.

McGrath, Susan. 2007. "The Vanishing." *Smithsonian Magazine,* February: http://www.smithsonianmag.com/science-nature/ vulture.html.

McManus, Phil. 2005. *Vortex Cities to Sustainable Cities: Australia's Urban Challenge.* Sydney: UNSW Press.

Merchant, Carolyn. 1995. *Earthcare: Women and the Environment.* London: Routledge.

Mission Australia, 2009. "Leading Charities Provide a New Start for ABC Learning." *Mission Australia/News,* http://www.probonoaustralia.com.au/news/2009/12/leading-charities-provide-new-start-abc-learning#.

Mitchell, Timothy. 1998. "Fixing the Economy." *Cultural Studies* 2(1): 82–101.

Mitchell, Timothy. 2008. "Rethinking Economy." *Geoforum* 39(3): 1116–1121.

Mollison, Bill. 1988. *Permaculture: A Designer's Manual.* Tyalgum, Australia: Tagari Publications.

Mollison, Bill. 1990. *Permaculture: A Practical Guide for a Sustainable Future.* Washington, DC: Island Press.

Morton, Timothy. 2007. *Ecology without Nature: Rethinking Environmental Aesthetics.* Cambridge: Harvard University Press.

Moss, Peter and Pat Petrie. 2002. *From Children's Services to Children's Spaces: Public Policy, Children and Childhood.*

London: Routledge.

Muecke, Steven. 1997. *No Road (Bitumen all the Way)*. Fremantle: Fremantle Arts Centre Press.

Murray-Darling Basin Authority. 2010. "Guide to the Proposed Basin Plan." Canberra: Murray-Darling Basin Authority.

Nancy, Jean-Luc. 2000. *Being Singular Plural,* Robert Richardson and Anne O'Byrne (trans). Stanford: Stanford University Press.

Oliveros, Pauline. 2005. *Deep Listening: A Composer's Sound Practice.* New York: iUniverse.

Pain, Deborah, Christopher Bowden, Andrew Cunningham, et al. 2008. "The Race to Prevent the Extinction of South Asian Vultures." *Bird Conservation International* 18: S30–S48.

Paxton, Steve. 1982. "Chute Transcript." *Contact Quarterly* 7 (Spring/Summer): 16–17.

Peattie, Lisa. 1998 "Convivial Cities." In *Cities for Citizens,* Mike Douglass and John Friedmann (eds), 247–253. Chichester: Wiley.

Perelman, Michael. 2000. *The Invention of Capitalism: Classical Political Economy and the Secret History of Primitive Accumulation.* Durham: Duke University Press.

Phillips, Andrea. 2005. "Walking and Looking." *Cultural Geographies* 12(4): 507–513.

Pinkstone, W.H. 2009. *Early Colonial Days: The Biography of a Reliable Old Native John McGuire.* Eugowra: Eugrowra Promotion and Progress Association.

Plumwood, Val. 1993. *Feminism and the Mastery of Nature.* London: Routledge.

Plumwood, Val. 2002. *Environment and Culture: The Ecological Crisis of Reason.* New York: Routledge.

Plumwood, Val. 2007. "Review of Deborah Bird Rose's *Reports from a Wild Country: Ethics for Decolonisation.*" *Australian Humanities Review* 42: 1–4.

Plumwood, Val. 2008. "Shadow Places and the Politics of Dwelling." *Australian Humanities Review* 44 (March): 139–150.

Plumwood, Val. 2009. "Nature in the Active Voice." *Australian Humanities Review* 46: 113–129.

Reynolds, Amanda, with Debra Couzens, Vicki Couzens, Lee Darroch, and Treahna Hamm. 2005. *Wrapped in a Possum Skin Cloak: The Tooloyn Koortakay Collection in the National Museum of Australia.* Canberra: National Museum Press.

Rigby, Kate. 2009. "Dancing with Disaster." *Australian Humanities Review* 46: 131–144.

Robbins, Paul. 1998. "Shrines and Butchers: Animals as Deities, Capital, and Meat in Contemporary North India." In *Animal Geographies: Place, Politics, and Identity in the Nature-Culture Borderlands,* Jennifer Wolch and Jody Emel (eds), 218–239. London: Verso.

Roelvink, Gerda. 2010. "Collective Action and the Politics of Affect, Emotion." *Space and Society* 3(2): 111–118.

Roelvink, Gerda and Magdalena Zolkos. 2011. "Climate Change as Experience of Affect." *Angelaki: Journal of the Theoretical Humanities* 16(4): 43–57.

Rose, Deborah Bird. 1999. "Indigenous Ecologies and an Ethic of Connection." In *Global Ethics and Environment,* Nicholas Low (ed), 175–188. London: Routledge.

Rose, Deborah Bird. [1992] 2000. *Dingo Makes Us Human: Life and Land in an Australian Aboriginal Culture.* Cambridge: Cambridge University Press.

Rose, Deborah Bird. 2004. *Reports from a Wild Country: Ethics for Decolonisation.* Sydney: UNSW Press.

Rose, Deborah Bird. 2005. "Rhythms, Patterns, Connectivities: Indigenous Concepts of Seasons and Change." In *A Change in the Weather: Climate and Culture in Australia,* Tim Sherratt, Tom Griffiths, and Libby Robin (eds), 32–41. Canberra: National Museum of Australia Press.

Rose, Deborah Bird and Thom van Dooren, eds. 2011. "Unloved Others: Death of the Disregarded in the Time of Extinctions" [special journal issue]. *Australian Humanities Review* 50: 1–178.

Rose, Deborah Bird, Diana James, and Christine Watson. 2003. *Indigenous Kinship with the Natural World in New*

South Wales. Hurstville: NSW National Parks and Wild-life Service.

Sandercock, Leonie. 2003. *Cosmopolis II: Mongrel Cities in the 21st Century.* London: Continuum.

Schafer, R. Murray. 1977. *The Turning of the World.* New York: Alfred A Knopf.

Shepard, Paul. [1973] 1998. *The Tender Carnivore and the Sacred Game.* Athens: University of Georgia Press.

Shiva, Vandana. 1991. *The Violence of the Green Revolution: Third World Agriculture, Ecology and Politics.* London: Zed Books.

Solnit, Rebecca. 2000. *Wanderlust: A History of Walking.* New York: Penguin Books.

Solnit, Rebecca. 2007. *Storming the Gates of Paradise: Land-scapes for Politics.* Berkely: University of California Press.

Somerville, Margaret. 2009. "Transforming Pedagogies of Water." In *Landscapes and Learning: Place Studies for a Global World,* Margaret Somerville, Kerith Power, and Phoenix de Carteret (eds), 207–224. Rotterdam: Sense Publishers.

Somerville, Margaret. 2013. *Water in a Dry Land: Place-learning through Art and Story.* Innovative Ethnography Series. London: Routledge.

Somerville, Margaret and Tony Perkins. 2010. *Singing the Coast.* Canberra: Aboriginal Studies Press.

Steffen, Will. 2009. "Surviving the Anthropocene" [video]. *BlipTV,* http://blip.tv/slowtv/surviving-the-anthropocene-prof-will-steffen-1974735.

Swan, Gerry, Vinaswan Naidoo, Richard Cuthbert, et al. 2006. "Removing the Threat of Diclofenac to Critically Endan-gered Asian Vultures." *PLOS Biology* 4(3): 395–402.

Turnbull, David. 2002. "Performance and Narrative, Bodies and Movement in the Construction of Places and Objects, Spaces and Knowledges: The Case of the Maltese Mega-liths." *Theory, Culture & Society* 19(5–6): 125–143.

Tyrell, James. 1933. *Australian Aboriginal-Place Names and their Meanings.* Sydney: Simmons Ltd.

UNICEF. 2005. *Cities with Children: Child Friendly Cities in*

Italy. Florence: UNICEF Innocenti Research Centre.

van Dooren, Thom. 2010. "Pain of Extinction: The Death of a Vulture." *Cultural Studies Review* 16(2): 271–289.

van Dooren, Thom. 2011a. *Vulture.* London: Reaktion Books.

van Dooren, Thom. 2011b. "Vultures and Their People in India: Equity and Entanglement in a Time of Extinctions." *Australian Humanities Review* 50: 45–61.

Volk, Tyler. 2003. *Gaia's Body: Toward a Physiology of Earth.* Cambridge: M.I.T. Press.

Watts, Jonathan. 2010. *When a Billion Chinese Jump: How China Will Save Mankind—or Destroy It.* London: Faber and Faber.

Weatherstone, John. 2003. *Lyndfield Park: Looking Back, Moving Forward.* Canberra: Worldwide Online Printing Braddon: http://lwa.gov.au/files/products/land-and-water-australia/pk030494/pk030494.pdf.

Weir, Jessica. 2009. *Murray River Country: An Ecological Dialogue with Traditional Owners.* Canberra: Aboriginal Studies Press.

Woodford, James. 2003. "The Swingers." *Sydney Morning Herald,* April 23: http://www.smh.com.au/articles/2003/04/23/1050777295349.html.

Worster, Donald. 1979. *Dust Bowl: The Southern Plains in the 1930s.* New York: Oxford University Press.

Wylie, John. 2005. "A Single Day's Walking: Narrating Self and Landscape on the South West Coast Path." *Transactions of the Institute of British Geographers* 30(2): 234–247.

Zournazi, Mary. 2002. *Hope: New Philosophies for Change.* Annandale, Australia: Pluto Press.

ABOUT THE AUTHORS

JENNY CAMERON is an Associate Professor in Geography and Environmental Studies at the University of Newcastle. She is a member of the Community Economies Collective and has been researching community economies for over fifteen years. She recently co-authored *Take Back the Economy: An Ethical Guide for Transforming our Communities* (with J.K. Gibson-Graham and Stephen Healy, 2013). She has produced community resources on topics that include Asset-Based Community Development and community gardening.[1]She is currently Chair of the Board of Directors of The Beanstalk Organic Food Cooperative.

RUTH FINCHER is a Professor of Geography at the University of Melbourne. An urban and social geographer, her research interests are in the politics of difference in cities and the role of institutions in influencing urban lives and places. Together with Kurt Iveson, she recently wrote *Planning and Diversity in the City: Redistribution, Recognition and Encounter* (2008).

J.K. GIBSON-GRAHAM is the pen-name of Katherine Gibson and the late Julie Graham, feminist political economists and economic geographers based at the Institute for Culture and Society, University of Western Sydney, Australia and the University of Massachusetts Amherst, USA. Their 1996 book *The End of Capitalism (As We*

[1]These resources are all available at http://www.communityeconomies. org/Resources/Community-Resources.

Knew It): A Feminist Critique of Political Economy was republished in 2006 by the University of Minnesota Press along with its sequel, *A Postcapitalist Politics*. They have co-edited collections with Stephen Resnick and Richard Wolff, *Class and Its Others* (2000) and *Re/Presenting Class* (2001). Julie and Kath are founding members of the Community Economies Collective.[2]

LESLEY INSTONE is a cultural geographer at the University of Newcastle, Australia. Her work focuses on Australian naturecultures and the multivalent entanglements of humans and non-humans. Recent research explores human-dog relations and urban public space, multispecies cohabitation in postcolonial lands, human-grassland relations, affective dimensions of ecological restoration, urban political ecology, and more-than-human methodologies.

KURT IVESON teaches urban geography at the University of Sydney. His research focuses on the relationship between cities and citizenship. He is the author of *Publics and the City* (Blackwell 2007) and co-author with Ruth Fincher of *Planning and Diversity in the City* (2008), and in 2010, he edited a special issue of the journal *City* on graffiti and street art (Volume 14, Issue 1). He is also author of the blog *Cities and Citizenship*,[3] and a Co-Chair of the Sydney Alliance's Transport Research-Action Team working to improve access to public transport across Sydney.

KUMI KATO is a Professor of Environmental Studies, Wakayama University, Japan and a Research Associate at the University of Queensland. As a member of an ecohumanities scholars group, Kangaloon, she defines herself as an ecohumanitarian activist, who believes in a "creative conservation" approach that attempts to build on strength, beauty, trust and the joy of being in this world.

GEORGE MAIN works as a Museum Curator and Environmental Historian at the National Museum of Australia. He is the author of *Heartland: The Regeneration of Rural Place* (2005) and *Gunderbooka: A "Stone Country" Story* (2000).

FREYA MATHEWS is an Adjunct Professor of Environmental Philoso-

---

[2] The Communities Economies Collective: http://www.community economies.org.

[3] *Cities and Citizenship*: http://citiesandcitizenship.blogspot.com.

phy at Latrobe University, Australia, where she co-coordinates the Environmental Culture Research Cluster. Her books include *The Ecological Self* (1991), *Ecology and Democracy* (editor, Routledge 1996), *For Love of Matter: A Contemporary Panpsychism* (2003), *Journey to the Source of the Merri* (2003), *Reinhabiting Reality: Towards a Recovery of Culture* (2005). She is the author of over sixty articles in the area of ecological philosophy and co-edits the journal, *Philosophy Activism Nature*. In addition to her research activities she manages a private biodiversity reserve in central Victoria.

ETHAN MILLER is a PhD student in Political and Social Thought at the University of Western Sydney and a member of the Community Economies Collective. His research focuses on rethinking concepts of ecology and economy in regional development processes, and on developing conceptual tools to strengthen post-capitalist grassroots organizing efforts. Ethan has written articles and developed popular education workshops around the concept and practice of "solidarity economics" and is active in a number of organizations, including the Clark Mountain Community Land Trust,[4] the Data Commons Cooperative,[5] and the JED Collective, a cooperative subsistence farm in Greene, Maine, USA.

ROBERT PEKIN started his working life as a dairy farmer in Victoria. After losing his dairy farm in 1998, he spend several years setting up traditional Community Supported Agriculture (CSA) projects around Australia (including his own CSA project on rented land near Hobart in Tasmania). But Robert dreamed of a larger CSA enterprise that would build a local and regional food system, and he's now done this for South East Queensland. Robert is passionate about living ethically on the planet, and is a frequent public speaker on topics that include sustainable food production, sustainable living and social enterprise.

KATE RIGBY is a Professor of Environmental Humanities at Monash University, and a Fellow of the Australian Academy of the Humanities and of the Alexander von Humboldt Foundation. Her research ranges across German Studies, European philosophy, literature and religion, and culture and ecology. Her books include *Topographies*

---

[4] The Clark Mountain Community Land Trust: http://www.clarkmoun tainclt.org.
[5] The Data Commons Cooperative: http://www.datacommons.coop.

of the Sacred: The Poetics of Place in European Romanticism (2004), *Ecocritical Theory: New European Approaches* (co-edited with Axel Goodbody, 2011), and *Dancing with Disaster: Environmental Histories, Narratives, and Ethics for Perilous Times* (2015). She is co-editor of the ecological humanities journal, *Philosophy Activism Nature*, and was the founding President of the Association for the Study of Literature and Environment (Australia-New Zealand).

GERDA ROELVINK is a lecturer in the School of Social Sciences and Psychology at the University of Western Sydney. Her research explores collective action centered on contemporary economic concerns, particularly climate change. She has published a range of articles in scholarly journals such as *Antipode, Emotion, Space and Society, Progress in Human Geography, Journal of Cultural Economy, Australian Humanities Review, Rethinking Marxism, Angelaki* and *Social Identities.* She is the co-editor with Kevin St. Martin of the forthcoming book *Making Other Worlds Possible: Performing Diverse Economies* (2015) and is the author of the forthcoming book *Geographies of Collective Action,* both being published by the University of Minnesota Press.

DEBORAH BIRD ROSE is a Fellow of the Academy of Social Sciences in Australia, and a founding co-editor of *Environmental Humanities.* Her current research interests focus on human-animal relationships in this time of extinctions, and she writes widely in both academic and literary genres. Her most recent book is *Wild Dog Dreaming: Love and Extinction* (2011). Other books include the re-released second edition of *Country of the Heart: An Indigenous Australian Homeland* (2011), the third edition of the prize-winning ethnography *Dingo Makes Us Human* (2009), *Reports from a Wild Country: Ethics for Decolonisation* (2004) and *Nourishing Terrains: Australian Aboriginal views of Landscape and Wilderness* (1996). She is an adjunct Professor in the University of New South Wales Environmental Humanities program, and author of the popular website *Life at the Edge of Extinction.*[6]

MARGARET SOMERVILLE is a Professor of Education and the Director of the Centre for Educational Research in the School of Education at the University of Western Sydney. She is a pioneer in place studies in Australia with a focus on the critical power of place in opening

---

[6] *Life at the Edge of Extinction:* http://www.deborahbirdrose.com.

spaces for alternative gendered, classed and ethnic stories to emerge. This has led to her development of alternative methodologies and modes of representation in educational research, and to consider the ways that these can be relevant and engaging for diverse local communities.

THOM VAN DOOREN is a Senior Lecturer in Environmental Humanities at the University of New South Wales, Australia. His current research focuses primarily on the ethical and political dimensions of extinction and conservation. He is the author of *Flight Ways: Life and Loss at the Edge of Extinction* (2014) and *Vulture* (2011). He is also co-editor of the journal *Environmental Humanities*.

JESSICA WEIR is a Senior Research Fellow at the Institute for Culture and Society, University of Western Sydney, and a Visiting Fellow at the Fenner School of Environment and Society at the Australian National University. She has published numerous journal articles and book chapters on water, native title, governance, and eco-philosophy, and is the author of *Murray River Country: An Ecological Dialogue with Traditional Owners* (2009). Her research is supported by research agreements and partnerships with Indigenous people in southeast Australia and the Kimberley.

ANNA YEATMAN is a Professorial Research Fellow in the Whitlam Institute at the University of Western Sydney. Recent publications include: *Individualization and the Delivery of Welfare Services* (2009), *State Security and Subject Formation* (co-edited with Magdaena Zolkos, 2010), and *Action and Appearance: Ethics and the Politics of Writing in Hannah Arendt* (co-edited with Phillip Hansen, Magdalena Zolkos and Charles Barbour, 2011).